THE BIG BOOK
OF SLOW COOKER RECIPES

Hundreds of Easy Recipes for your Crockpot

Compiled by
Trevor J Ponting

Compiled and edited by Trevor J Ponting
Copyright © 2009 Trevor J Ponting
Published and printed by Lulu Press Inc.
ISBN 978-1-4092-6948-9

CONTENTS

THE BIG BOOK OF SLOW COOKER RECIPES

FISH AND SEAFOOD

LAMB

PORK

POULTRY

VEGETARIAN

DESSERTS

INTRODUCTION

The slow cooker, also known as the crockpot, is making a big comeback -- and the timing couldn't be better. Our lives are busier, crazier, more stressed than ever. We want our meals to be fuss-free, yet we still yearn for home-cooked, long-simmered, rich flavours. The new crockpots satisfy both desires. With just 10 minutes of preparation time, you can come home eight to 10 hours later to a sensational, nutritious dinner. All you have to do is lift the crockpot lid and serve. (Don't worry if you're running late: the meal will be fine if it slow-cooks for 10-12 hours; in fact, flavours improve over time.)

Unlike the old slow cookers, the new units are loaded with practical improvements and fashion-forward exteriors (like the one on the front of this book). The look is streamlined and sleek, and the stainless-steel and white-enamel models stand proud on any kitchen work-top. They also have removable crockery, so you can take the inner pot right to the table, and then straight to the dishwasher (some slow cookers are also safe in the oven and microwave and on the stove). Sold in both round and oval shapes, slow cookers are available in a variety of sizes -- perfect for feeding two or 10. And, the new "keep warm" setting on some models is great for parties where guests arrive at different times.

With these 21st-century crockpots, you'll want some contemporary recipes -- ones that are delicious and easy to prepare. The recipes which I have included in this book are just that! Quickly prepare dinner the night before and sit down to a hearty meal.

Trevor Ponting
Quick Brown Fox Publications
London, NW5
March, 2009.

BEEF

ALL DAY CROCKPOT DELIGHT

1.5 kg. boneless stewing steak, cut into 1 inch cubes
50 grams flour
1 onion, sliced
1 teaspoon salt
1/8 teaspoon pepper
1 clove garlic, crushed
500 ml. beer
30 grams flour

Coat beef cubes with the 50 grams flour. Brown in melted butter. Drain off excess fat. In crockpot, combine browned meat with onion, salt, pepper, garlic and beer. Cover and cook on low 5-7 hours (all day) until meat is tender. Turn control to high. Dissolve remaining 30 grams flour in small amount of water. Stir into meat mixture, cook on high 30-40 minutes. Serve with rice and salad.

ALMOST LASAGNA

900 grams pasta , uncooked
2 x family-sized jars pasta sauce with tomato chunks
1 egg
225 grams minced beef
225 grams sausage
2 tablespoons olive oil
225 grams parmesan cheese
115 grams Italian breadcrumbs
1 bag mozzarella cheese
570 grams. Ricotta cheese
2 eggs
225 grams parmesan cheese
1½ teaspoons parsley flakes
dash salt & pepper

Grease crockpot, or spray with non-stick cooking spray. Cook pasta according to packet directions, drain. Brown and drain meat. Toss pasta with olive oil. Add pasta sauce to mixture, toss well. Stir together parmesan cheese, breadcrumbs, egg, 1/2 bag mozzarella cheese, and browned meat. If you wish, you can sprinkle lightly with garlic powder. Beat together ricotta, 2 eggs, parmesan, parsley, salt & pepper. Pour half of pasta/sauce/meat mixture into crockpot. Spread entire ricotta mixture over first layer of pasta. Cover ricotta layer with remaining pasta mixture, and cover with remaining cheese. Cover, and cook on low 4-6 hours.

APPLE AND BROWN SUGAR CORNED BEEF

1 corned beef brisket
950 ml. apple juice
225 grams brown sugar
1 tablespoon prepared mustard
8 small red potatoes
2 medium carrots, pared and cut into chunks
1 onion, peeled and cut into eights
1/2 head cabbage, cut into chunks

Place all ingredients in large crockpot (cut meat in half if necessary). Stir to mix. Cook on high for 4 to 5 hours on high or 8 to 10 hours on low. Remove meat and vegetables and some of the cooking liquid. Slice meat thinly across the grain.
Serve with the vegetables and some of the liquid. Use left over corned beef the next day.....layer in crockpot with sauerkraut and Swiss cheese. Warm and serve on rye bread with thousand island dressing!

BARBEQUE BEEF STEW

900 grams stewing meat
3 tablespoons oil
1 onion, sliced
1/2 green pepper, chopped
1 large clove garlic
½ teaspoon salt
1/8 teaspoon pepper
500 ml. beef stock
1 can tomatoes
1 can mushrooms
80 ml. barbecue sauce
2 teaspoons cornflour
60 ml. cold water

Sauté onion, pepper and garlic in oil. Add salt, pepper, beef stock, tomatoes, mushrooms and barbecue sauce. Cook in crockpot on low heat 8-10 hours. Mix cornflour, cold water and thicken before serving. Serve over hot cooked rice.

BARBECUE BRISKET

First, make a batch of homemade barbecue sauce:
1 tablespoon liquid smoke
1 tablespoon crushed garlic
1 large onion, chopped
2 tablespoons cider vinegar
1 tablespoon loose brown sugar (not packed)
3 tablespoons fresh squeezed lemon juice
1 medium-sized bottle tomato ketchup
½ teaspoon chilli powder
4 tablespoons Worcestershire sauce
1 tablespoon dry mustard powder (like Coleman's)
250 ml. water or red wine
1 teaspoon salt
1/8 teaspoon black pepper
1 tablespoon honey

Mix together and heat on hob. Then prepare the brisket by removing all silver skin if the butcher didn't already do this, place it in the crockpot, pour the homemade sauce over it and cook on low. The length of time cooking will depend on how large a brisket you are using. When done, remove lid from crockpot and using two forks shred the brisket. Terrific served on rolls or buns. It's also good served like tacos with all the trimmings in soft or regular taco shells.

BARBECUE SAUCE

150 grams chopped celery
1 medium onion, chopped
1 tablespoon butter
2 tablespoons vinegar
1 tablespoon brown sugar
3 tablespoons Worcestershire sauce
1 tablespoon lemon juice
1 teaspoon salt (optional)
1 teaspoon mustard
250 ml. ketchup
250 ml. water
900 grams minced beef

Combine all ingredients in a large saucepan. Cook slowly for 2 to 2½ hours. (is better reheated)

BARBECUE STEAK

675 grams boneless stewing steak,
1 ½ inches thick
1 clove garlic, peeled and crushed
60 ml. wine vinegar
1 tablespoon brown sugar
1 teaspoon paprika
2 tablespoons Worcestershire sauce
120 ml. ketchup
1 teaspoon salt
1 teaspoon dry or prepared mustard
¼ teaspoon black pepper

Cut the beef on a diagonal, across the grain into slices 1 inch wide. Place these in the crockpot. In a small bowl, combine the remaining ingredients. Pour over the meat, and mix. Cover and cook on Low for 3 to 5 hours.

BARBECUED COCKTAIL MEATBALLS

907 grams lean minced beef
400 ml. ketchup, divided
3 tablespoons seasoned dry bread crumbs
1 egg, slightly beaten
2 tablespoons dried onion flakes
¾ teaspoon garlic salt
½ teaspoon black pepper
200 grams packed brown sugar
1 can tomato paste
65 ml. reduced-sodium soy sauce
65 ml. cider vinegar
1 ½ teaspoons hot pepper sauce

Preheat oven to 350 °F. Combine minced beef, 80 ml. ketchup, bread crumbs, egg, onion flakes, garlic salt and black pepper in medium bowl. Mix lightly but thoroughly; shape into 1-inch meatballs. Place meatballs in two 15 x 10 inch Swiss roll tins or shallow roasting pans. Bake for 18 minutes or until browned. Transfer meatballs to slow cooker. Mix remaining 250 ml. ketchup, sugar, tomato paste, soy sauce, vinegar, and hot pepper sauce in medium bowl. Pour over meatballs. Cover and cook on low for 4 hours. Serve with cocktail picks.
Makes about 4 dozen meatballs.

BARBECUED MEATBALLS

1 kg. minced beef
600 grams bread crumbs
1 teaspoon garlic powder
2 sachets onion soup mix
2 teaspoons Worcestershire sauce
2 eggs

Sauce:
2 onions, chopped
325 ml. tomato paste

2 cloves garlic, crushed
60 ml. Worcestershire sauce
60 ml. red wine vinegar
110 grams brown sugar
120 ml. sweet pickle relish
120 ml. beef broth
2 teaspoons salt
2 teaspoons dry mustard

Combine first 6 ingredients and mix well. Shape into meatballs and brown in a frying pan with 1 tablespoon of oil. Drain on paper towels. Add all sauce ingredients to crockpot and stir well. Add meatballs and cook, covered, on low for 5 to 6 hours (high for 2 to 3). Serve from the crockpot. Makes about 60 meatballs.

BEEF AND BEANS

1 x 910 gram can stewing beef
1 tablespoon prepared mustard
1 tablespoon taco seasoning
½ teaspoon salt
¼ teaspoon pepper
2 garlic cloves, crushed
1 x 450 gram can diced tomatoes, un-drained
1 medium onion, chopped
1 can kidney beans, rinsed and drained
1 can chilli beans

Combine mustard, taco seasonings, salt, pepper and garlic in a large bowl. Add beef and toss to coat. Put the beef in your crockpot and add the rest of the ingredients. Cover and cook for 6 -8 hours on low. Serve over hot rice.

BEEF BOURGUIGNON

240 ml. dry red wine
2 tablespoons olive oil
1 large onion -- sliced
1/2 teaspoon thyme
2 tablespoons parsley - chopped
1 bay leaf
1/4 teaspoon pepper
900 grams stewing beef, cut into 1 1/2-inch cubes
3 slices bacon, diced
12 small white onions
230 grams sliced mushrooms
2 cloves garlic -- minced
1 teaspoon salt

Combine first seven ingredients, mix well, add beef. Marinate at least 3 hours (overnight if refrigerated) Drain meat, reserving marinade. In frying pan, Sauté bacon and remove. Brown meat in bacon fat. Combine beef, bacon, vegetables and seasonings in slow cooker. Pour over enough marinade to cover. Cook on low 8-10 hours.

BEEF BURGUNDY

2 slices bacon -- chopped
900 grams sirloin steak -- cut in 1 inch cubes
30 grams flour
1 teaspoon salt
1/2 teaspoon seasoned salt
1/4 teaspoon marjoram
1/4 teaspoon thyme
1/4 teaspoon pepper
1 clove garlic -- minced
1 cube beef stock -- crushed
250 ml. Burgundy wine
2 tablespoons cornflour

In large frying pan cook bacon several minutes. Remove bacon and set aside. Coat beef with flour and brown on all sides in bacon mixture. Combine steak, bacon drippings, cooked bacon, seasonings, stock and Burgundy in crockpot. Cover and cook on low for 6 to 8 hours or until meat is tender. Turn control to high. Add cornflour (dissolved in 2 tablespoons water); cook on high 15 minutes. Serves 6.
NOTES : Can add ¼ pound fresh mushrooms during last 15 minutes, if desired.

BEEFBURGER STROGANOFF

1.9 kilos lean minced beef
3 slices bacon, diced
1 small onion, chopped
2 tablespoons flour
¼ teaspoon paprika
1 teaspoon salt
1 large can condensed cream of mushroom soup
2 tablespoons dry red wine
250 ml. sour cream
6 to 8 hamburger buns, toasted and buttered

In large frying pan, brown beef and bacon until red colour disappears. Drain. In crockpot, mix together drained beef, bacon, onion, flour, paprika, and salt. Stir in undiluted soup and wine. Cover pot and cook on low 4 to 5 hours. Stir in sour cream. Spoon mixture over toasted buns. Serves 6 to 8.

BEEF BURGUNDY

2 slices bacon, chopped
900 grams sirloin steak, cut in 1- inch cubes
30 grams flour
1 teaspoon salt
½ teaspoon seasoned salt
¼ teaspoon marjoram
¼ teaspoon thyme
¼ teaspoon pepper
1 clove garlic, crushed
1 cube beef stock, crushed
250 ml. Burgundy wine
2 tablespoons cornflour

In large frying pan cook bacon several minutes. Remove bacon and set aside. Coat beef with flour and brown on all sides in bacon mixture. Combine steak, bacon drippings, cooked bacon, seasonings, stock and Burgundy in crockpot. Cover and cook on low for 6 to 8 hours or until meat is tender. Turn control to high. Add cornflour (dissolved in 2 tablespoons water); cook on high 15 minutes. Serves 6.
NOTES : You can add 1/4 pound fresh mushrooms during last 15 minutes, if desired.

BEEF 'N' BREW VEGETABLE SOUP

3 medium onions, sliced
450 grams carrots, cut into ½ inch slices
4 parsnips, cut into ½ inch slices
2 bay leaves
4 cloves garlic, crushed
1 tablespoon snipped fresh thyme or 1 teaspoon dried thyme, crushed
½ teaspoon pepper
2 tablespoons quick-cooking tapioca
1.9 kilos beef stew meat, cut into 1 inch cubes

1 x 400 gram can beef broth
1 x 340 gram can beer

In a large crockpot, place onions, carrots, parsnips, garlic, bay leaves, dried thyme, and pepper. Sprinkle with tapioca. Place meat on top of vegetables. Add beef broth and beer. Cover; cook on low-heat setting for 10 to 12 hours or on high-heat setting for 5 to 6 hours. To serve, remove bay leaves; if using fresh thyme, stir in now.

BEEF FAJITAS

1.9 kilos beef flank steak
150 grams chopped onion
1 green sweet pepper, cut into ½ inch pieces
1 jalapeno pepper, chopped
1 tablespoon cilantro
2 garlic cloves, crushed (or ¼ teaspoon garlic powder)
1 teaspoon chilli powder
1 teaspoon ground cumin
1 teaspoon ground coriander
½ teaspoon salt
1 can (230 grams) chopped tomatoes
12 x 8-inch flour tortillas
Toppings: sour cream, guacamole, grated cheddar cheese and salsa

Cut steak into 6 portions. In any size crockpot combine meat, onion, green pepper, jalapeno pepper, cilantro, garlic, chilli powder, cumin, coriander and salt. Add tomatoes. Cover and cook on low 8-10 hours or high 4-5 hours. Remove meat from crockpot and shred. Return meat to crockpot and stir. To serve, spread meat mixture into flour tortillas and top with toppings. Roll up.

BEEF ROGAN JOSH

450 grams sliced stewing steak
1 large onion, fairly thinly sliced
3 garlic cloves, sliced
3 tablespoons rogan josh curry paste
1 can plum tomatoes
1 tablespoon mango chutney
2 tablespoons creamed coconut
6 ounces small mushrooms, quartered
3 tablespoons canola oil
1 beef stock cube
1½ cups boiling water

Brown onions in frying pan using canola oil. Add garlic and fry for a further 3 minutes. Add curry paste and fry off for 2 minutes. Place mixture into crockpot. De-glaze pan with boiling water and add to crockpot. Add the rest of the ingredients except mushrooms and cook on high setting for 2 hours, then on low setting for 6-8 hours.
Add mushrooms and check seasoning. Cook on high setting for a further ½ hour. Skim off excess fat before serving. Serves 2 to 4.

BEEF STEW (1)

907 grams stewing beef
60 grams flour
1 teaspoon paprika
4 large carrots
3 large potatoes
250 ml. condensed beef broth
1½ teaspoons salt
½ teaspoon pepper
85 ml. soy sauce
1 large onion
1 can tomato sauce (225 grams.)

Layer potatoes, then carrots. Top with meat; sprinkle meat with soy sauce, salt, paprika, pepper and flour. Spread with chopped onions. Combine beef broth and tomato sauce and pour over all. Cover and cook on low 7 - 8 hours or high 4 - 5 hours.

BEEF STEW (2)

450 grams. beef bourguignon (or cheaper cut)
3 large sweet potatoes (cut into 1 inch thick slices)
2 cans beef stock (or broth or consommé)
2 small cans tomato paste
3-4 handfuls of assorted vegetables (eg. frozen beans and carrots)
450 grams. fresh mushrooms (quartered)
1 large onion (diced)
2 cloves garlic (crushed)
30 grams flour

Mix bite-sized pieces of meat in flour, brown in some oil along with the crushed garlic. While meat is browning, combine beef stock and tomato paste in a crockpot, mix well. Pre-cook the sweet potatoes until just tender, add to crockpot along with onions and any raw vegetables that you may use. Add enough water to cover and cook on low for as long as for about 5 hours. Add the frozen vegetables and some quartered mushrooms during the last 1 hour or so. Thicken with a little flour and water, let it cook another 15 minutes uncovered, and serve.

BEEF STROGANOFF (1)

910 grams steak, sliced thin across the grain
450 grams fresh mushrooms, sliced
1 medium onion, sliced
¼ teaspoon thyme
180 ml. dry sherry
180 ml. beef broth
¾ teaspoon dry mustard
¼ teaspoon garlic salt

Put all ingredients in the crockpot, stir well and cook on low for 8 hours. Turn heat to high and mix 1½ cups sour cream and ½ cup flour, heat on high for 40 minutes. Serve over rice or noodles.

BEEF STROGANOFF (2)

1.4 kilos beef steak, ½ inch thick
115 grams flour
2 teaspoon salt
1/8 teaspoon pepper
½ teaspoon dry mustard
2 medium onions, thinly sliced and separated into rings
2 x 115 gram cans sliced mushrooms, drained or 1.9 kg. mushrooms, sliced
1 x 300 gram can condensed beef broth
60 ml. dry white wine (optional)
375 ml. sour cream
60 grams flour

Trim all excess fat from steak and cut meat into 3 inch strips about ½ inch wide. Combine 50 grams flour, the salt, pepper and dry mustard; toss with steak strips to coat thoroughly. Place coated steak strips in crockpot; stir in onion rings and mushrooms. Add beef broth and wine; stir well. Cover and cook on low setting for 8 to 10 hours. Before serving, combine sour cream with 30 grams flour; stir into crockpot. Serve stroganoff over rice or noodles.

BEEF TACO BEAN SOUP

900 grams stewing beef
1 packet taco seasoning
1 can Mexican style diced tomatoes (425 grams)
1 small can green chillis
1 x 225 gram can tomato sauce
1 onion, chopped
2 beef Oxo cubes
2 x 425 gram cans red kidney beans, rinsed, drained
grated cheddar cheese

Cut roast into bite-sized chunks. Roll in taco seasoning and add to crockpot. Then add the tomatoes, chillis, tomato sauce, onion, and stock cubes. Cover and cook on low setting for 6 hours or until meat is tender. Add the drained beans and cook until the beans are heated through; around

30 minutes. Serve topped with cheese, and/or the toppings that you like.

BEEF TIPS

115 grams flour
1 teaspoon salt
1/8 teaspoon pepper
1.8 kilos beef or sirloin tips
115 grams chopped green onions
225 grams mushrooms, sliced
1 x 300 gram can condensed beef broth
1 teaspoon Worcestershire sauce
2 teaspoons tomato paste or ketchup
65 ml. dry red wine or water
3 tablespoons flour
buttered noodles

Combine 50 grams flour with the salt and pepper and toss with beef cubes to coat thoroughly. Place in crockpot. Add green onions and drained mushrooms. Combine with beef broth, Worcestershire sauce and tomato paste or ketchup. Pour over beef and vegetables; stir well. Cover and cook on low setting for 7 to 12 hours. One hour before serving, turn to high setting. Make a smooth paste of red wine and 3 tablespoons flour; stir into crockpot, mixing well.

BEER MEATBALLS

1 can of beer
1 teaspoon lemon juice
1 teaspoon hot sauce
30 grams breadcrumbs
190 grams onions
salt and pepper to taste
1 large bottle ketchup
1 teaspoon horseradish
1 teaspoon Worcestershire sauce
900 grams to 1350 grams minced beef
2 to 3 eggs

Combine minced beef, 120 grams onions, Italian bread crumbs, eggs. Make the mixture into small meatballs. Then fry or bake the meat. In a saucepan combine remaining ingredients. Simmer for 15 minutes. Put meatballs and sauce into crockpot. The sauce should cover the meat. Allow to simmer in slow cooker for at least 3 hours, however, the longer you let them simmer, the better they are! 6 to 10 hours on a low setting is great! Stir them occasionally. You may wish to add more ketchup, or spice them up if you like them hot.

BRUNCH CASSEROLE

675 grams minced beef
1 large onion, finely chopped
2 tablespoons olive oil or butter
2 garlic cloves, crushed
1 can mushrooms, sliced and drained (or use sautéed fresh mushrooms instead)
2 teaspoons salt
½ teaspoon nutmeg
½ teaspoon oregano
½ packet spinach -- chopped
3 tablespoons flour
6 eggs, beaten
65 ml. milk -- scalded
115 grams mature cheddar cheese, grated

In frying pan, lightly brown minced beef and onion in olive oil; drain well. Place in well-greased crockpot. Stir in remaining ingredients except eggs, milk and cheese until well blended. Beat eggs and milk together. Pour over other ingredients; stir well. Dust with additional nutmeg. Cover and cook on low setting for 7 to 10 hours or until firm. Just before serving, sprinkle with grated cheese. Makes 6 to 8 servings.

CABBAGE AND BEEF CASSEROLE

910 grams minced beef
1 head cabbage, grated
1 small onion, chopped
1 x 450 gram can tomatoes
broth or tomato juice to cover bottom of pot
garlic salt, thyme, red pepper and a dash of oregano

Brown minced beef and drain. Shred cabbage and chop onion. Put in broth or other liquid to cover bottom of pot. Layer cabbage, onion, spices, meat, and garlic salt. Repeat layers ending with beef. Top with un-drained tomatoes and a dusting of oregano. Cook on high setting for 1 hour. Stir all together. Cook on low setting for 8 to 10 hours, until ready to eat. Makes 3-4 servings.

CABBAGE BURGER BAKE

900 grams grated cabbage and carrots
340 grams lean minced beef
½ teaspoon salt
¼ teaspoon ground black pepper
1 medium onion, finely chopped
225 grams long-grain rice
1 large can chunky low-fat spaghetti sauce
120 ml. water
¼ teaspoon dried basil leaves, crushed
¼ teaspoon seasoned salt

Place half of the cabbage and carrots in a slow cooker. Crumble minced beef over top. Sprinkle ¼ teaspoon of the salt and 1/8 teaspoon of the pepper. Evenly distribute onion, then rice over all. Top with remaining cabbage, salt, and pepper. Combine spaghetti sauce, water, basil, and seasoned salt; pour over cabbage. Cover and cook on low setting for 5 to 6 hours or until rice is tender.

CARNE GISADA

1.5 kilos stewing beef
2 cans diced tomatoes with green chillis
salt and pepper to taste
3 cloves garlic, crushed
150 grams chopped onion
3 tablespoons flour
½ teaspoon cumin
½ teaspoon oregano
1 teaspoon chilli powder
60 ml. water
1 diced bell pepper

Place stewing beef, 60 ml. water, salt and pepper in crockpot. Turn heat to high setting and simmer for 1½ hours. Drain juice from tomatoes into measuring cup. Add tomatoes garlic and onions to crockpot. Stir. Simmer on high setting for 30 minutes. Add cumin, oregano, and chilli powder to crockpot and stir again. Blend juice and enough water to equal 350 ml. of liquid and flour stir into meat and vegetable mixture. Cook on low for 3-4 hours until sauce thickens. Serve with warm flour tortillas.

CHEESE AND MEATBALL SOUP

500 ml. water
150 grams corn (whole kernel)
150 grams potatoes, chopped
150 grams celery, chopped
120 grams carrots, sliced
120 grams onions, chopped
2 cubes beef stock
1 x 450 gram jar cheese sauce

Meatballs

450 grams minced beef
60 grams breadcrumbs
1 large egg
½ teaspoon salt
½ teaspoon Tabasco sauce

Mix the meatball ingredients together thoroughly. Shape into medium size meatballs. Place uncooked meatballs and all other ingredients, except cheese sauce, in slow cooker. Stir gently. Cover and cook on low setting for 8 to 10 hours. Before serving add cheese sauce, stirring gently until well blended.
Serve with crusty bread. Serves 6.

CHILLI

900 grams minced beef
1 large onion
1 large green pepper
1 large jalapeno pepper
Chilli powder to taste
Garlic salt to taste
Salt to taste
Pepper to taste
Sugar to taste
2 cans crushed tomatoes
1 can tomato puree
1 can kidney beans
2 cans hot chilli beans

Brown beef. Sauté chopped onion and green pepper in oil. Mix beef, onion and green pepper. Add spices; allow to stand 1 hour. Add tomatoes, tomato puree, beans. Cook in crockpot all day. Best if refrigerated and warmed the next day.

CHILLI (2)

2 onions, chopped
2 cloves garlic
450 grams. lean hamburger mince
2 tablespoon. chilli powder
cumin to taste
2 x 450 gram cans tomatoes
2 cans tomato soup
2 cans kidney beans, drained
salt and pepper to taste
grated cheese and/or sour cream for
topping (optional)

Cook onions and garlic in 2 tablespoons oil till onions are yellow. Add hamburger mince and cook till browned. Stir in chilli powder and optional cumin; cook 2 minutes more. Meanwhile, in crockpot, combine remaining ingredients. Stir in browned meat mixture. Cover and cook on low setting for 8-10 hours. To serve: ladle chilli into bowls. Top with optional grated cheese and/or sour cream, if desired.

CHILLI BEEF DIP

1 x 312 gram can condensed chilli beef soup
1 x 85 grams packet cream cheese, softened
120 ml. sour cream
1 tablespoon water
1 teaspoon prepared mustard
1 teaspoon Worcestershire sauce
½ teaspoon chilli sauce
¼ teaspoon hot pepper sauce, optional

In crockpot, combine all ingredients; mix well. Cover and cook on low for 1½ to 2 hours, stirring occasionally, or until cheese is melted and dip is hot.

Serve warm with tortilla or corn chips. Makes 500 ml.

CHILLI , CHEESE AND TACO DIP

450 grams. hamburger
1 can chilli (no beans)
450 grams. mild cheese, cubed or grated

Brown hamburger; drain and place in slow cooker. Add chilli and cheese; cover and cook on low until cheese is melted (about 1 to 1½ hours, stirring occasionally to blend ingredients. Serve warm with taco or tortilla chips.

CHILLI CON CARNE

1.8 kg. minced beef
3 tablespoons shortening
160 grams chopped onion
2 garlic cloves, crushed
4 tablespoons chilli powder
3 beef stock cubes, crushed
1½ teaspoons paprika
1 teaspoon oregano
1 teaspoon ground cumin
½ teaspoon cayenne pepper
120 ml. beef stock
1 can tomatoes
1 can tomato paste
4 cans red kidney beans

Heat shortening in frying pan and brown beef, discard fat. Combine all ingredients in crockpot. Cover and cook on low setting for 8-10 hours; high setting for 4-5 hours or auto setting for 6-7 hours.

CHILLI DIP

1 large jar mild piquant sauce
2 cans refried beans
225 grams sour cream
½ teaspoon chilli powder
450 grams minced beef
1 onion, chopped
salt and pepper to taste
225 grams. cheddar cheese, grated
jalapenos or mild chilli, chopped, to taste

Cook minced beef with onion; drain. Mix everything together in crockpot and cook slowly. Serve with favourite vegetables or chips.

CHILLI WITH 4 KINDS OF BEANS

1 kg. browned minced beef
2 cans hot chilli beans
2 cans dark red kidney beans, drained
2 cans pinto beans, drained
2 cans kidney beans, drained
2 cans tomatoes
1 packet chilli seasoning

Put all ingredients in crockpot and cook on low for about 10 hours).

CHINESE PEPPER STEAK

910 grams boneless beef steak
1 clove garlic, crushed
½ teaspoon salt
¼ teaspoon pepper
60 ml. soy sauce
1 tablespoon hosin sauce
1 teaspoon sugar
1 tomato, seeded, peeled & diced
2 red or green bell peppers, cut into strips
3 tablespoons cornflour
3 tablespoons water
150 grams fresh bean sprouts
4 green onions, finely chopped
cooked rice

Trim fat from steak; slice into thin strips. Combine steak, garlic, salt, pepper, soy sauce, hosin sauce and sugar in slow cooker. Cover and cook on low setting for about 4 hours. Turn control to high. Add tomato and bell peppers. Dissolve cornflour with water in a small bowl and stir into steak mixture. Cover and cook on high for 15-20 minutes or until thickened. Stir in bean sprouts, sprinkle with onions. Serve with rice. Serves 4–6.

CHINESE PIE

800 grams minced beef
165 grams diced green and red bell peppers
165 grams diced onion
Gravy granules, eg. Bisto, to taste
4 to 6 medium red or round white potatoes, diced
2 tablespoons butter, melted
1 x 425 gram can whole kernel corn, drained
1 x 425 grams can creamed corn
salt and pepper to taste

Brown minced beef with diced peppers and onion. Drain well. Place minced beef mixture in crockpot. Toss diced potato with melted butter to coat and add to crockpot; add whole kernel corn and creamed corn. Salt and pepper to taste. Cover and cook on low setting for 7 to 9 hours. Taste and adjust seasonings. Serves 4 to 6.

CHOW MIEN

1 x 115 gram can mushrooms
1 kilo cubed steak
4 stocks celery
2 medium onions
250 ml. hot water with 3 stock cubes
3 tablespoons soy sauce
2 teaspoons Worcestershire sauce
1 x 450 gram. can Chinese vegetables
2 tablespoons cornflour and 2 tablespoons water

Cook for 8 to 10 hours in crockpot. One hour before serving add Chinese vegetables, cornflour and water.

CORNED BEEF AND CABBAGE

1 kilo corned beef brisket
2 medium onions, quartered
1 cabbage head, cut in small wedges
½ teaspoon pepper
3 tablespoon. vinegar
3 tablespoon. sugar
240 ml. water

Combine ingredients in removable liner with cabbage on top. Cut meat to fit, if necessary. Place liner in base. Cover and cook on low 10-12 hours, high 6-7 hours, or auto 6-8 hours. Serves 6.

CORNED BEEF HASH

1 can of corned beef
1 medium onion, grated
2 medium celery sticks, chopped
5 fair sized potatoes chopped
2 tablespoons butter
1 diced green pepper
3 cloves garlic (or to your taste)
150 grams mushrooms
1 tablespoon Worcestershire sauce
a dash or two of Italian seasoning

salt and pepper to taste
2 x 285 grams cans of chicken broth

Grind or chop your corned beef and toss it in the crockpot with all the other ingredients in the list above. Cook on low setting for 8 hours. When the potatoes are well cooked, mash them in the pot and add a little water if needed. Then serve it with warm bread and salad!

CRANBERRY COCKTAIL MEATBALLS

900 grams minced beef
120 grams cornflake crumbs
2 eggs
120 grams chopped, fresh parsley
85 grams ketchup
3 tablespoons minced onions
2 tablespoons soy sauce
¼ teaspoon garlic powder
¼ teaspoon pepper sauce
1 x 4 450 gram can cranberry sauce
340 grams chilli sauce
1 tablespoon brown sugar
1 tablespoon lemon juice

In a large bowl, combine minced beef, cornflake crumbs, parsley, eggs, ketchup, onion, soy sauce, garlic powder and pepper. Mix well and form into small balls, from ½ inch to ¾ inch in diameter. Place in a casserole or baking pan. Heat oven to 300°F. Meanwhile in a saucepan, combine cranberry sauce, chilli sauce, brown sugar and lemon juice. Cook stirring over medium heat until smooth. Pour hot sauce over meatballs in casserole. Bake for 30 to 45 minutes, depending on the size of the meatballs. Transfer to Crockpot and keep on low for serving.

CROCKPOT ROAST

1 kg. chuck roast
2 packets dry Italian dressing mix
250 ml. water

Place beef in crockpot, sprinkle seasonings over meat, pour water over all. Cook on low setting for 6-8 hours or until meat shreds easily.

FRENCH DIP

1 x 2.25 kilo rump roast
1 tablespoon garlic powder
1 tablespoon black pepper
1 teaspoon seasoning salt
1 teaspoon oregano
½ teaspoon rosemary
2 Oxo cubes
2 cans beef broth
1 large onion, diced

Place all ingredients in a crock pot. Cook on high setting for 5-6 hours or low setting for 8-10. Remove the meat from the crockpot and place on a deep plate-to collect juices. Strain the broth well so that it is clear and no spices or onions remain. Place in a saucepan and keep warm. Most people prefer to keep the broth as is but you can stir in a small amount of cornflour mixed with cold water to thicken it up just a touch. (Remember to add the juices that drain off the meat) Heat buns to warm and slice the meat thin.

FAVOURITE CROCKPOT CHILLI

900 grams coarsely minced beef steak
2 x 450 gram cans red kidney beans, drained
2 x 400 grams cans tomatoes, drained
2 medium onions, coarsely chopped
1 green pepper, seeded and coarsely chopped

2 cloves garlic, peeled and crushed
2-3 tablespoons chilli powder
1 teaspoon black pepper
1 teaspoon cumin
salt and pepper to taste

In a large, preferably non-stick saucepan brown the meat and drain off the fat. Put the minced beef and other ingredients in a large crockpot. If you have a small crockpot, cut the recipe in half. Stir well. Cover and cook on low setting for 10-12 hours.

FRANKS IN SPICY TOMATO SAUCE

250 ml. ketchup
120 grams firmly packed brown sugar
1 tablespoon red wine vinegar
2 teaspoons soy sauce
1 teaspoon Dijon mustard
1 clove garlic, crushed
450 grams beef or chicken frankfurters, cut into 1 inch pieces

Place ketchup, brown sugar, vinegar, soy sauce, mustard, and garlic in the crockpot. Cover and cook on High until blended. Stir occasionally. Add frankfurters and stir to coat. Cook until thoroughly blended. Serve with toothpicks or wooden skewers to spear franks.

GLAZED COCKTAIL SAUSAGES

165 grams apricot preserves
60 ml. prepared yellow mustard
2 scallions, chopped
230 grams precooked mini smoked sausages

In a slow cooker; mix together the preserves and mustard. Stir in scallions and sausages. Cover, and cook for 3 hours or until very hot. Remove the cover, stir to mix and serve immediately with toothpicks; keep the heat on for another 30-60 minutes if desired while serving.

GRAPE JAM MEATBALLS

350 ml. chilli sauce
225 grams grape jam (or currant jam)
1 to 3 teaspoons Dijon mustard
450 grams lean minced beef
1 egg, lightly beaten
3 tablespoons fine dry bread crumbs
½ teaspoon salt

Combine chilli sauce, jam, and mustard in Crockpot and stir well. Cook, covered, on high setting while preparing meatballs. Combine remaining ingredients and mix thoroughly. Shape into 30 meatballs. Bake meatballs in a preheated 400 degree oven for 15 to 20 minutes; drain well. Add meatballs to sauce, stir to coat, cover and cook on low setting for 6 to 10 hours.

GREEK STEW

1.4 kg. of stewing beef
7 small onions
3 cloves garlic, crushed
1 large can tomatoes
120 ml. beef stock
1 x 340 gram can tomato paste
2 tablespoon red wine vinegar
2 teaspoon dried oregano
½ teaspoon each of salt and pepper
55 grams flour
120 ml. cold water
1 sweet green pepper, chopped
120 grams crumbled feta cheese
2 tablespoon. chopped fresh parsley

Cut beef into 1 inch cubes, trimming off any fat. Cut onions into wedges leaving root end intact. Put meat and onions into slow cooker along with garlic and tomatoes. Combine beef stock, vinegar, oregano, salt and pepper and add to slow cooker, stirring gently to blend. Cook on low setting for 8-9 hours or High for 6 hours. Add flour and water mixture and chopped green pepper. Cook on high setting for 15 minutes or until thickened. Serve sprinkled with feta and parsley.

HAMBURGER CASSEROLE

1 kg. browned minced beef
3 carrots, peeled and sliced
2 onions, sliced
4 potatoes, peeled and sliced
1 can peas, drained
2 stalks celery, diced
1 can cream of chicken soup
1 can water

Place potatoes in bottom of crockpot, top with carrots and other vegetables. Place minced beef on top. Combine soup and water and pour over minced beef. Cover and cook on low for 6 to 8 hours.

HAMBURGER DIP

900 grams lean minced beef
150 grams chopped onion
2 cloves garlic, crushed
salt to taste
2 cans tomato sauce
120 grams ketchup
1½ teaspoons oregano
2 teaspoons white granulated sugar
2 x 8 oz. packets cream cheese, softened and cut in cubes
170 grams grated Parmesan cheese
1 teaspoon mild chilli powder

In frying pan, brown minced beef with onion, discard fat. Pour browned meat and onion into slow cooker. Add garlic, salt, tomato sauce, ketchup, oregano, sugar, cream cheese, Parmesan cheese and chilli powder. Set crockpot on low setting until cream cheese has melted and is thoroughly blended (1½ to 2 hours). Stir, taste and adjust seasoning if desired. Serve with cubed French bread or tortilla chips. If spicier dip is desired, use hot chilli powder in place of mild chilli powder. Finely chopped jalapenos may be added, if desired.

HAMBURGER-SAUSAGE DIP

450 grams minced steak
250 ml. piquant sauce
1 can cream of mushroom soup
900 grams cheese, cut into pieces
450 grams pork sausage
1 teaspoon garlic powder
1 can tomatoes
¾ teaspoon oregano

Combine piquant sauce, garlic powder, soup, tomatoes, oregano and cheese in crockpot. Brown minced meat and sausage until it is done. Drain very well and place in slow cooker. Cook on low until cheese is melted. Serve with your favourite chips.

HEARTY BEEF DIP

225 grams cream cheese, cubed
35 grams sliced dried beef, diced
2 tablespoons green onion, chopped
60 ml. milk
60 grams pecans, chopped
1 garlic clove

Combine cream cheese and milk in greased crockpot. Cover and heat until cheese is melted (30 to 60 minutes). Add remaining ingredients and stir thoroughly. Cover and heat for 30 minutes. Serve with crackers or bread pieces.

HOT DOG HORS D'OEUVRES

900 grams all beef hot dogs, sliced in half
450 grams. bacon, sliced in half
brown sugar

Wrap each hot dog half with bacon strip. Fasten with toothpick. Layer in slow cooker/Crockpot, sprinkling each layer with a thin layer of brown sugar. Repeat layers until hot dogs run out. Cook on low for 2-3 hours, stirring gently with wooden spoon every 30 minutes.

HUNGARIAN GOULASH

680 grams stewing beef, cut into 1- inch cubes
1 large onion, chopped
2 small cloves garlic, crushed
½ teaspoon salt
½ teaspoon pepper
125 ml. water
2 tablespoons tomato paste
2 tablespoons sweet paprika
75 grams flour
125 ml water
125 ml. cup sour cream
hot cooked buttered noodles, tossed with poppy seeds

Place beef in slow cooker; add onion and garlic. Sprinkle with salt and pepper. Combine water, tomato paste, and paprika; pour over beef mixture. Cover and cook on low setting for 8 to 9 hours. Combine flour, water, and sour cream or yogurt; stir into meat mixture. Cook, uncovered, on high setting for 15 minutes or until slightly thickened. Serve with buttered noodles tossed with poppy seeds. Serves 4 to 6.

LASAGNA

1 packet pepperoni slices
450 grams. hamburger
1 onion, diced
1 green pepper, diced
1 can mushrooms
1 packet noodles
1 large jar pizza sauce
1 large jar spaghetti sauce
1 packet grated Mozzarella cheese

Cook together hamburger, onion, green pepper and mushrooms. Layer this with the rest of the ingredients in the crockpot. Cook on high setting for 2 to 3 hours.

LITTLE SMOKIES

2 packets cocktail frankfurters
1 medium bottle chilli sauce
1 medium jar grape jam

Combine in crockpot and cook on low setting for 6 to 8 hours.

MANHATTAN MEATBALLS

450 grams minced beef
450 grams. mild pork sausage
500 grams soft bread crumbs or
115 grams oatmeal
2 eggs
115 grams chopped onion
2 tablespoons parsley
2 teaspoons salt
½ teaspoon garlic salt

Sauce:
1 x 340 gram jar apricot preserves
125 ml. barbecue sauce

Mix first 8 ingredients together and form meatballs. Brown in frying pan or in the oven at 450° F. for 15 minutes. Heat sauce, pour over meatballs. Bake at 350°F for 25 minutes or cook in crockpot. Can be served over rice or as an appetiser with toothpicks. Makes 4 or 5 dozen.

MEATBALLS

900 grams hamburger mince
120 grams breadcrumbs
1 egg
grated parmesan cheese
parsley and oregano
onion and garlic powder
milk
1 can beer
1 bottle ketchup, regular size

Mix hamburger mince, breadcrumbs, egg, seasonings and milk together. Make small meatballs. Bake the meatballs to eliminate most of the greast, then mix ketchup and beer in the crockpot and simmer for several hours.

MEXICAN CHILLI

2 x 450 gram cans red kidney beans, drained
1 large can tomatoes, cut up
225 grams chopped celery
225 grams chopped onion
1 x 170 gram can tomato paste
115 grams chopped green pepper
1 x 115 gram can green chilli peppers, drained and chopped
2 tablespoons sugar
1 bay leaf
½ teaspoon garlic powder
1 teaspoon salt
1 teaspoon dried, crushed marjoram
dash of pepper
450 grams. minced beef

In frying pan brown minced beef

and drain. In slow cooker combine all ingredients. Cover, cook on low heat for 8 to 10 hours. Remove bay leaf and stir before serving. Makes about 10 servings and is great with corn bread!

MINCED BEEF STROGANOFF

900 grams minced beef
2 medium onions, chopped
2 cloves garlic, crushed
1 can sliced mushrooms, drained
1½   teaspoons salt
¼ teaspoon pepper
1 cup beef stock or consommé
3 tablespoons tomato paste
2 tablespoons flour
¾ cup sour cream, mixed with the flour

Brown minced beef in large frying pan; add onions, garlic and mushrooms. Sauté until onion is golden brown. Put in crockpot with all remaining ingredients except sour cream and flour. Stir thoroughly. Cover and cook on low setting for 6-8 hours (or on high setting for 3 hours). Stir in sour cream and flour 1 hour before serving. Serve over hot buttered noodles or rice. Serves 6 - 8

NO-BEAN CHILLI

900 grams minced beef, or cubed lean stewing beef
1 x 225 gram can tomato sauce
1 x 170 gram can tomato paste
1 x 450 gram can stewed tomatoes (optional)
2 tablespoons chilli powder
1½ teaspoons salt
1 teaspoon (or more) hot pepper sauce

Combine all ingredients in slow cooker. Cover and cook on low setting for 8-10 hours. Serves 4 to 6.

PARTY HAMBURGER DIP

450 grams hamburger
700 grams cheddar cheese
1 can tomatoes and chillis
½ onion, diced
340 grams fresh mushrooms, sliced

Brown hamburger, mushrooms and onion; drain. Melt cheese in slow cooker. Add remaining ingredients and simmer on high setting for about 30 minutes. Serve with corn chips or crackers. Turn crockpot to low while serving.

PIQUANT CHEESE DIP

700 grams minced beef, browned
1 x 310 gram can cream of mushroom soup
900 grams processed cheese
110 grams margarine
1 onion, chopped
2 tablespoons chilli powder
250 ml. piquant sauce

Brown meat and onion. Drain. Add all ingredients to slow crockpot and cook on low heat until cheese melts, (about 1½ hours). Serve in slow crockpot with tortilla chips.

PIZZA FONDUE

450 grams. minced beef
2 cans pizza sauce with cheese
225 grams grated cheddar cheese
225 grams grated Mozzarella
1 teaspoon oregano
½ teaspoon fennel seed
1 tablespoon cornflour

Brown minced beef and drain. Add all other ingredients. Place in slow cooker and heat through. Serve with tortilla chips.

REUBEN DIP

1 small can sauerkraut
225 grams cream cheese
170 grams grated Swiss cheese
170 grams diced corned beef
2 tablespoons thousand island dressing

Drain and rinse sauerkraut, mix with cream cheese and Swiss cheese. Add diced corned beef and Thousand Island dressing. Cover and heat on low setting until cheeses are melted, stirring occasionally to blend all ingredients. Serve warm with crackers or cocktail rye bread.

SOUR CREAM CHILLI BAKE

450 grams minced beef
1 x 425 gram can pinto beans, drained
1 x 285 gram can enchilada sauce
1 x 225 gram can tomato sauce
125 grams grated processed cheese
1 tablespoon instant minced onion
250 ml. water
300 grams corn chips
250 ml. sour cream

120 grams grated processed cheese

Brown minced beef; drain. Transfer meat to crockpot. Stir in beans, enchilada sauce, tomato sauce, 125 grams of cheese, onion and 250 ml. of water. Reserve 225 grams of corn chips; crush the remaining chips and add to the meat mixture. Cover and cook on low setting for 8 to 10 hours. To serve, top with sour cream, remaining cheese, and reserved corn chips.

SPAGHETTI SAUCE

4 tablespoons cooking oil
1 small onion, finely chopped
1 x 450 gram can tomato sauce
240 ml. water
½ teaspoon pepper
½ teaspoon red pepper (optional)
450 grams minced beef
1 can tomato purée
1 can tomato paste
1 teaspoon salt
½ teaspoon oregano
900 grams sausage

Brown minced beef in 2 tablespoon hot oil in frying pan. When almost browned, add onion and continue browning until onion is tender. Pour meat and onion into 3½ quart crockpot. Add purée, sauce, paste, water, salt, pepper and oregano and set dial on low setting. Cut 907 grams sausage into pieces and brown in remaining 2 tablespoons oil. When brown, place sausages in sauce in crockpot. Continue cooking for 12 hours. (If you like your sauce sweeter, you could add 100 grams sugar to this.)

SPICY DIP

910 grams cheese
910 grams hamburger, cooked and drained
1 large jar Old El Paso taco sauce
1 large onion, chopped fine

Mix all together in crockpot where cheese will melt and everything will keep warm.

SPICY MARMALADE MEATBALLS

Meatballs:
910 grams minced beef
120 grams bread crumbs
1 teaspoon Worcestershire sauce
1/2 teaspoon salt
¼ teaspoon pepper
1 small onion, finely chopped
½ teaspoon chilli powder
¼ teaspoon garlic powder
3 eggs

Sauce:
500 ml. ketchup
60 ml. Worcestershire sauce
1 jar orange marmalade (340 grams)
dash cayenne, more or less to taste
1 teaspoon chilli powder

Combine sauce ingredients in slow crockpot; cover and cook on high setting while preparing meatballs. Combine meatball ingredients. Heat a large frying pan over medium high heat. Add meatballs; brown on all sides. You might have to do this in batches. Place browned meatballs in a 325° oven and bake for 45 minutes (if the frying pan isn't oven-proof, transfer to a baking dish). Transfer meatballs to slow cooker with a slotted spoon or drain on brown paper first. Cover and reduce to low setting for 2 to 4 hours. Serve hot as an appetizer or over rice for a main dish. Makes 24 to 48 meatballs, depending on size.

SPICY FRANKS

250 ml. ketchup
60 grams brown sugar, packed
1 tablespoon red wine vinegar
2 teaspoons soy sauce
2 teaspoons Dijon mustard
1/8 teaspoon garlic powder
450 grams hot dogs, cut into bite-size pieces, or cocktail frankfurters, smoked sausage, etc.

Combine everything but hot dogs in the crockpot; cover and cook on high setting for 1 to 2 hours, until well blended. Add hot dogs, stir, and cook for another 1 to 2 hours, until heated through. Turn to low to keep warm and serve from the crockpot.

SWEET AND SOUR FRANKS

250 ml. chilli sauce
225 grams currant jam
3 tablespoons lemon juice
1 tablespoon prepared mustard
900 grams cocktail franks or hot dogs cut into bite-sized pieces
2 large cans pineapple chunks

Combine first four ingredients in crockpot and mix wel. Blend sauce ingredients, cover and cook on high setting for 15 to 20 minutes. Add cut-up hot dogs or cocktail franks and pineapple. Cover and cook on high setting for 2 hours; or on low setting for 4 hours. Keep on low while serving.

SWISS STEAK

900 grams rump steak
2 tablespoons flour
1 sliced green pepper
1 teaspoon salt
1/8 teaspoon pepper
2 tablespoons salad oil
1 large onion, sliced
1 x 450 grams can tomatoes, cut up
1 stalk celery, thinly sliced
1 tablespoon thick bottled steak sauce

Cut steak into serving size pieces. Coat with flour, salt and pepper. In large frying pan or a slow cooker with a browning unit, brown meat in oil. Pour off excess fat. In slow cooker, combine meat with tomatoes, onion, green pepper and steak sauce. Cover and cook on low setting for 6 to 8 hours or until tender. Thicken juices with additional flour, dissolved in a small amount of water, if desired. Makes 5 or 6 servings. Serve with mashed potatoes.

TACO CHILLI

900 grams lean minced beef
1 medium onion, chopped
1 sachet taco seasoning mix
2 x 410 gram cans diced tomatoes
1 x 284 gram can diced tomatoes with green chillis
1 x 450 gram can pinto beans, rinsed and drained
1 x 425 gram can chilli beans in sauce
150 grams frozen whole kernel corn
grated cheese
slightly crushed tortilla chips

In a large frying pan, cook minced beef and onion, one half at a time, until meat is browned and onion is tender. Drain off fat. Transfer to a 3 ½ - to 5-quart slow cooker. Stir in dry taco seasoning mix, diced tomatoes, diced tomatoes with green chillies, pinto beans, chilli beans in chilli sauce, and corn. Cover and cook on low setting for 8 to 10 hours or on setting high for 4 to 5 hours. Sprinkle each serving with some cheese and chips. Makes 8 servings.

TEXAS CHILLI

6 strips bacon
907 grams boneless beef cubes
2 x 425 gram cans kidney beans, drained
1 large can tomatoes, cut up
1 x 225 gram can tomato sauce
225 grams finely chopped onion
115 grams thinly sliced carrots
115 grams finely chopped green pepper
115 grams finely chopped celery
2 tablespoon. minced parsley
2 cloves garlic, crushed
1 bay leaf
2 tablespoons chilli powder
1 teaspoon salt
1/8 teaspoon pepper

Fry bacon until crisp. Remove bacon and drain on paper towel. Brown half the beef cubes in pan with bacon dripping for five minutes. Place in slow cooker. Repeat with remaining meat. Stir bacon and remaining ingredients into 3½ quart slow cooker. Cover and cook on low setting for about 10 hours or until beef is tender. Stir occasionally.

VEGETABLE BEEF SOUP

450 grams minced beef
150 grams chopped onion
1 large can whole tomatoes (chopped)
450 grams diced potatoes
1 x 450 gram can cut green beans
2 teaspoon chilli powder
2-3 dashes cayenne pepper sauce
2 x 300 gram cans condensed beef stock
150 grams chopped celery
150 grams sliced carrots
1 teaspoon salt
1 teaspoon Worcestershire sauce

Brown meat with onion and celery; drain off fat. Stir in remaining ingredients and add 500 ml. water. Cover and cook on low setting for 8 to 10 hours.

FISH AND SEAFOOD

AFRICAN FISH STEW

2 whole fish - tilapia, bream, bass or similar
flour - to coat fish
salt, black pepper
4 tablespoons vegetable oil
2 onions, finely chopped
1 can tomatoes, chopped
1 tablespoon tomato puree
125 ml fish stock or water
cayenne pepper to taste

Cut the fish into sections to fit into the crockpot. Season the flour and coat each piece of fish. Heat the oil in a frying pan and quickly fry each piece of fish - then put the fish into the crockpot. Fry the onions until softened and mix in the tomatoes, tomato puree and stock or water. Bring the sauce to the boil and taste - season with cayenne. Pour the sauce over the fish and cook on low setting for 4 to 6 hours.

ATHENIAN SHRIMP IN TOMATO AND FETA SAUCE

2 tablespoons olive oil
1 medium onion, chopped
1 clove garlic, crushed
2 cans tomatoes
1 can tomato puree
6 oz. tomato paste
¼ cup dry wine
2 tablespoons parsley, finely chopped
1 teaspoon dried oregano
¼ teaspoon fresh ground pepper
1 kilo shrimps, peeled and drained
60 grams feta cheese, cut into ¼ inch cubes

Heat oil and add the onion and garlic. Cook, stirring often, until the onion is softened (about 4 minutes). Transfer to a slow cooker. Add the tomatoes with their purée, the tomato paste, wine, parsley, oregano and pepper. Cover and cook for 6 to 8 hours on low setting . Increase the heat to high and add the shrimp. Cook just until the shrimp are firm and have turned pink (about 15 minutes). Stir in the feta cheese and serve immediately.

BAYOU GUMBO

3 tablespoons flour
3 tablespoons oil
250 grams smoked sausage, cut into ½ inch slices
300 grams okra, chopped
1 large onion, chopped
1 large green bell pepper, chopped
3 garlic cloves, crushed
¼ teaspoon ground cayenne pepper
¼ teaspoon pepper
1 can diced tomatoes, un-drained
1 medium packet frozen prawns
300 grams uncooked regular long-grain white rice
700 ml. water

In a small saucepan, combine flour and oil; mix well. Cook, stirring constantly over medium-high heat for 5 minutes. Reduce heat to medium; cook, stirring constantly, about 10 minutes or until mixture turns reddish brown. Place flour-oil mixture in 3 slow cooker. Stir in all remaining ingredients except prawns, rice and water. Cover, and cook on low setting for 7-9 hours. When ready to serve, cook rice in water as directed on packet. Meanwhile, add prawns to gumbo mixture in slow cooker and mix well. Cover, and cook on low setting for additional 20 minutes. Serve gumbo over rice. Makes 6 servings.

CHEESY TUNA-STUFFED POTATOES

4 medium or large potatoes, scrubbed and left dripping wet
75 grams finely-grated cheddar cheese
65 ml. milk
1 can tuna in water, drained
125 ml. sour cream
1 green onion, thinly sliced

Try this for a light lunch or supper. Prick each dripping wet potato with a fork; add potatoes to a slow cooker (do not add water). Replace lid and cook on low setting for 6-8 hours until fork tender. Remove potatoes from cooker using tongs; cut them in half lengthwise; scoop out the center of each half with a big spoon, leaving enough potato to keep the shell intact. Put the potato pulp in a bowl and add ½ cup cheese, milk, tuna, sour cream, and green onion. Mash the filling with a fork; spoon mixture back into shells, mounding high. Return to slow cooker, placing the stuffed potatoes in a single layer if possible so that they touch each other. Sprinkle with the remaining ¼ cup cheese. Cover and cook on high setting for 45 minutes to 1 hour. Remove carefully and serve.

CHUNKY VEGETABLE CLAM CHOWDER

2 cans minced clams
500 grams peeled potatoes, cut into ½ inch cubes
225 grams finely chopped onion
225 grams chopped celery
1 teaspoon sugar
¼ teaspoon salt
¼ teaspoon pepper
2 cans condensed cream of potato soup
240 ml. water
225 grams non-fat dry milk powder
85 grams flour
250 ml. cold water

4 slices bacon, crisply cooked, drained, and crumbled
paprika

Drain clams, reserving liquid. Cover clams, and chill. In crockpot combine reserved clam liquid, potatoes, onion, celery, carrot, sugar, salt, and pepper. Stir in potato sour and 500 ml. water. Cover; cook on low heat for 8 to 10 hours or on high heat for 4 to 5 hours. If using low heat setting, turn to high. In a medium bowl combine non-fat dry milk powder and flour. Gradually whisk in 250 ml. cold water; stir into soup. Cover; cook on high setting 10 to 15 minutes or till thickened. Stir in clams. Cover; cook 5 minutes more. Ladle soup into bowls. Sprinkle each serving with crumbled bacon and paprika. Makes 6 to 8 servings.

CITRUS FISH

910 grams fish fillets
salt and pepper to taste
1 medium onion, chopped
5 tablespoons chopped parsley
4 teaspoons oil
2 teaspoons grated lemon rind
2 teaspoons grated orange rind
orange and lemon slices

Butter slow cooker and put salt and pepper on fish to taste. Then place fish in pot. Put onion, parsley and grated rinds and oil over fish. Cover and cook on low for 1 ½ hours. Serve garnished with orange and lemon slices.

CLAM CHOWDER

4 x 180 grams) cans clams
910 grams salt pork or bacon, diced
1 large onion, chopped
6 to 8 large potatoes, pared and cubed
750 ml. water
3½ teaspoons salt
¼ teaspoon pepper
1 litre single cream or milk
3 to 4 tablespoons cornflour

Cut clams into bite sized pieces if necessary. In a frying pan sauté salt pork or bacon and onion until golden brown. Drain. Put into crockpot with clams. Add all remaining ingredients, except milk. Cover, and cook on high setting for 3 to 4 hours or until potatoes are tender. During the last hour of cooking, combine 250 ml. of milk with the cornflour. Add that and the remaining milk and stir well. Heat through. Serve in large bowls with crusty French bread.

COCONUT THAI SHRIMP AND RICE

2 cans chicken broth
1 cup water
1 teaspoon ground coriander
1 teaspoon ground cumin
1 teaspoon salt
½ teaspoon cayenne pepper
grated zest of 2 limes
1/3 cup lime juice
7 cloves garlic, crushed
1 tablespoon grated fresh ginger
1 medium onion, chopped
1 red bell pepper, diced
1 peeled carrot, grated
56 grams flaked coconut
112 grams sultanas
400 grams white rice
450 grams jumbo shrimps, peeled and de-veined
56 grams fresh sugar snap peas, cut into thin strips
toasted coconut for garnish

In a large slow cooker, mix the chicken broth, water, coriander, cumin, salt, cayenne pepper, lime zest, lime juice, garlic, and ginger. Stir in the onion, bell pepper, carrot, coconut, raisins, and rice. Cover and cook on the low heat setting for 3½ hours, or until the rice is just tender. Stir in the shrimp and sugar snap peas. Cover and cook 30 minutes longer. Serve garnished with toasted coconut. Serves 6.

CRAB DIP

450 grams. cheese
450 grams. butter or margarine
2 cans crab meat

Heat together. Keep warm in fondue or slow crockpot. Serve with bread sticks.

EEL IN RED WINE WITH SAGE AND BACON

8 pieces of eel - 3 to 4 inches each
2 tablespoons lemon juice
2 tablespoons vegetable oil
300 ml. red wine
1 large onion, peeled and chopped
2 tablespoons fresh parsley
whole sage leaves
bacon rashers - enough to wrap the eel
1 egg yolk
2 tablespoons cream

Put the eel into a dish and pour over the lemon juice, oil, wine, onion and parsley. Leave to marinate for an hour or so. Remove the eel from the marinade and wrap in sage leaves and then bacon. Either place these pieces with the join side down into your crockpot or skewer with a cocktail stick or tie with string. Then pour the marinade over the pieces. Cook on low setting for 4 to 6 hours. Combine the cream and egg yolk and mix into the sauce, then allow it to reheat for 15 minutes or so. If you prefer, you could thicken the sauce with cornflour or arrowroot

FISH IN TOMATO SAUCE

150 grams white fish steaks or fillets
1 x 400 gram can peeled Italian plum
tomatoes - chopped
1 tablespoon tomato puree
garlic salt to taste
fresh ground black pepper
1 diced green pepper

Turn the crockpot onto low. Stir the tomato purée into the chopped tomatoes, season and add the green pepper. Lay the fish fillets in the bottom and pour over the tomato mixture. Leave to cook for 3 to 5 hours on low setting, or 2 to 3 hours on high setting if you prefer.

JAMAICAN FISH

1 kilo of fish - tilapia, snapper, bass
1 medium onion - peeled and chopped
2 tablespoons soy sauce
2 sprigs of thyme or 1 teaspoon dried
50 grams butter
1 tablespoon flour
oil for frying
2 tablespoons tomato puree

Set the crockpot to low. Heat the oil in a frying pan and fry the fish to seal. Place it in the bottom of the crockpot. Melt the butter in the same pan and fry the onion until soft then add the flour and mix to a roux. Slowly stir in the soy sauce and cook for a couple of minutes, stirring all the time. Stir in approximately 450ml of fish stock or a mixture of water and wine. Add the tomato purée, thyme and season to taste. Pour on the sauce over the fish and cook for 4 hours. The fish you choose for this Jamaican fish recipe will depend on what's available - serve it with rice and peas or maybe boiled sweet potato.

MARINER FONDUE

2 cans condensed cream of celery soup
500 grams grated sharp processed cheese
225 grams chunked cooked lobster
115 grams chopped cooked prawns
115 grams chopped cooked crabmeat
60 grams. finely chopped, cooked scallops
dash paprika
dash cayenne pepper
1 loaf of French bread, cut into 1 inch cubes

Combine all ingredients except bread cubes in lightly greased crockpot. Stir thoroughly. Cover and cook on high setting for 1 hour or until cheese is melted. Turn to low setting for serving. Using fondue forks, dip bread cubes into fondue. Makes about 3 pints.

PRAWNS CREOLE

300 grams diced celery
160 grams chopped onion
300 grams chopped bell pepper
1 x 230 gram can tomato sauce
1 large can whole tomatoes
1 clove garlic (1 teaspoon garlic salt or ¼
teaspoon garlic powder may be substituted)
1 teaspoon salt
¼ teaspoon pepper
6 drops Tabasco sauce (optional)
450 grams prawns, de-veined and shelled

Combine all ingredients except prawns. Cook 3 - 4 hours on high setting or 6 - 8 hours on low. Add prawns during last hour of cooking. Serve over hot rice. Chicken, rabbit or crawfish may be substituted for the prawns.

PRAWN MARINARA

1 x 450 gram can of tomatoes, cut up
2 tablespoons crushed parsley
1 clove of garlic, crushed
½ teaspoon dried basil
1 teaspoon salt
¼ teaspoon pepper
1 teaspoon dried oregano
1 x 170 gram can tomato paste
1/2 teaspoon seasoned salt
50 grams cooked shelled prawns
grated parmesan cheese
cooked spaghetti

In a crockpot, combine tomatoes with parsley, garlic, basil, salt, pepper, oregano, tomato paste and seasoned salt. Cover and cook on low setting for 6 to 7 hours. Turn control to high, stir in prawns, cover and cook on high for 10 to 15 minutes more. Serve over cooked spaghetti. Top with Parmesan cheese.

SALMON WITH SWEET CHILE GLAZE

4 salmon steaks
1 Serrano chili, seeded and chopped
1 garlic clove, crushed
2 tablespoons brown sugar
1 tablespoon soy sauce
2 teaspoons lime zest
2 tablespoons lime juice
2-3 teaspoons sweet chili sauce
1 tablespoon honey (optional)
fresh cilantro stems, for garnish
lime wedges, for garnish

Preheat the crockpot to high. Lightly rinse salmon, set aside. Stir together the chilli, garlic, brown sugar, soy, lime zest and juice and chili sauce. Place salmon in the crockpot and pour the sauce over the top. Cover, reduce heat to low setting and cook for 2-3 hours. If you want a stickier glaze, pour the cooking liquid into a small saucepan, add the honey and boil for 3 minutes. Garnish with cilantro and lime wedges and serve. Serves 4.

SALMON AND POTATO CASSEROLE

4 potatoes, peeled and thinly sliced
3 tablespoons flour
salt and pepper
1 x 450 gram can salmon, drained and flaked
1 medium onion, chopped
1 x 305 gram can cream of mushroom soup
60 ml. water
nutmeg

Place half of the potatoes in a greased slow cooker. Sprinkle with half of the flour, salt and pepper. Cover with half the salmon; sprinkle with half the onion. Repeat layers in order. Combine soup and water. Pour over potato-salmon mixture. Dust with nutmeg. Cover and cook on low setting for 7-10 hours. Serves 6.

SALMON BAKE IN CROCKPOT

3 x 450 gram cans salmon
10 slices soft bread, crumbed
1 x 450 gram can tomatoes in purée
1 green pepper, chopped
3 teaspoons lemon juice
1 can condensed cream of onion soup
2 chicken stock cubes, crushed
6 eggs, well beaten
1 can condensed cream of celery soup
120 ml. milk

Grease removable liner well. Combine all ingredients, except celery soup and milk, in removable liner. Place liner in base. Cover and cook on low setting for 4-6 hours or auto for 3 hours. Combine cream of celery soup with 120 ml. of milk and heat in saucepan. Use as sauce for salmon bake.

SEAFOOD CHOWDER

450 grams fish fillets
125 grams bacon - diced
1 onion - peeled and diced
450 grams potatoes - peeled and diced
600 ml. milk
600 ml. water
1 bay leaf
1 tablespoon Worcester sauce

Heat the slow cooker to low while you're preparing the ingredients. Fry the bacon bits in a pan until the fat runs - then add the potato and fry for 5 minutes or so until beginning to soften. Add the onions and fry a further 5 minutes - add a little oil if necessary. Transfer these to the crockpot. Cut the fish into chunks, add them to the pot with the rest of the ingredients. Cook on low setting for about 5 hours. Serve with crusty bread for a lovely hearty seafood chowder.

SOUSED HERRINGS

8 herrings
salt and pepper
1 onion, peeled and cut into rings
8 whole black peppercorns
fresh parsley
1 bay leaf
150ml. vinegar
150 ml. water

Clean and gut the herrings, removing the heads, tails and fins. Turn them so that the inside of the fish is facing your worktop and press down hard with the heel of your hand. This will loosen the backbone for you to remove it prior to cooking. Season with salt and pepper, add a slice of onion and roll up from the tail end - secure with a wooden stick and pack tightly in the bottom of the crockpot. Put the onions and other ingredients into a saucepan and bring to the boil. Pour the mixture over the fish and cook on low setting for 4 to 5 hours. You can either eat them hot or leave them to cool in the sauce. This method can be adapted for soused mackerel or pilchards and the liquid can be cider, pale ale or white vinegar substituted for the ordinary vinegar. Experiment with the combinations to develop your own pickled fish recipe.

SWEET AND SOUR PRAWNS

1 x 170 gram packet frozen Chinese pea pods, partially thawed
1 x 368 gram can pineapple chunks (drain and reserve juice)
2 tablespoons cornflour
3 tablespoons sugar
1 chicken stock cube
250 ml. boiling water
120 ml. reserved pineapple juice
2 teaspoon soy sauce
½ teaspoon ground ginger
2 x 128 gram cans prawns, rinsed & drained
2 tablespoons cider vinegar
fluffy rice

Place pea pods and drained pineapple in crockpot. In a small saucepan, stir together cornflour and sugar. Dissolve stock cube in boiling water and add with juice, soy sauce and ginger to saucepan. Bring to the boil, stirring, and cook sauce for about 1 minute or until thickened and transparent. Gently blend sauce into pea pods and pineapple. Cover and cook on low setting for 4 to 6 hours. Before serving, add prawns and vinegar, stirring carefully to avoid breaking up prawns. Serve over hot rice. Makes 4 to 5 servings.

TROUT IN WINE SAUCE

oil for greasing
4 trout
110 grams mushrooms, sliced
150 ml white wine
1 lemon - grated rind and juice
freshly ground black pepper
1/4 teaspoon salt
150ml double cream, crème fraiche or soured cream

Grease the crockpot with a little olive oil and place the gutted and headed trout tail to head in the bottom of the crockpot. Add the sliced mushrooms, wine, lemon rind and juice, a twist of black pepper and salt. Put the lid on the crockpot and cook on low setting for about 3 to 4 hours. Stir in the crème fraiche or cream or soured cream and heat a further 15 minutes or so. This would be lovely served with some new potatoes, green beans and cauliflower - all lightly steamed.

TUNA NOODLE CASSEROLE

2 cans cream of celery soup
80 ml. dry sherry
170 grams milk
2 tablespoons parsley flakes
300 grams peas
2 cans tuna, drained
300 grams egg noodles, cooked
2 tablespoons butter or margarine
dash curry powder (optional)

In a large bowl, thoroughly combine soup, sherry, milk, parsley flakes, vegetables, and tuna. Fold in noodles. Pour into greased crockpot. Dot with butter or margarine. Cover and cook on low setting for 7 to 9 hours. (Cook noodles until just tender.)

TUNA SALAD CASSEROLE

2 cans tuna, drained and flaked
1 can cream of celery soup
4 hard-biled eggs, chopped
150 grams diced celery
120 ml. mayonnaise
¼ teaspoon pepper
2 small bags ready-salted potato crisps, crushed

Combine all ingredients except 60 grams of the crushed potato chips; stir well. Pour into greased crockpot. Top with remaining potato crisps. Cover and cook on low setting for 5-8 hours.

LAMB

BO-PEEPS-A-CROCK

1 x 1.4 kilo veal/lamb breast
2 tablespoons chicken stock mix, combined
in a litre of water
1 teaspoon nutmeg
1 teaspoon ginger, powdered
16 cloves, whole
1 medium/large carrot, chopped
1 cup grapes (optional)

Cut the meat as needed to fit in the slow cooker, removing as much fat as possible. Now toss in the rest. Cook on high setting for 4 hours, then cool it and skim off the fat. Reheat and it's good heated for 6 hours at a shot for 2 days. (refrigerate in between times!) Tastes delicious with an acorn or butternut squash, cut in half and baked then served in a bowl with the shell filled with meat and soup. Add Basmati or Jasmine rice for a perfect but easy meal.

BRAISED LAMB SHANKS WITH BARLEY

4 x 225 gram lamb shanks
2 tablespoons olive oil
3 fresh garlic cloves (or 1 tsp. garlic powder)
1 medium onion, chopped fine
2 bay leaves
½ teaspoon dried thyme
1 pinch nutmeg (optional)
2 tablespoons salt
150 grams pearl barley
1 can tomatoes, chopped
1 tablespoon tomato paste
250 ml. water
250 ml. dry red wine, such as burgundy

In a heavy frying pan, brown lamb shanks in hot olive oil. Remove shanks and set aside. Sauté onion, garlic and spices in oil until onion is soft. Transfer the entire dish to the crockpot. Add salt, barley, tomatoes, tomato paste, water (and wine if desired) to shanks. Make sure all the barley is immersed in liquid. Cook on low setting for at least 8 hours. Turn off the heat and let the dish sit uncovered for 10-20 minutes. Use a tablespoon and skim off any excess fat from the top before serving. Serves 4.

CURRIED LAMB AND RISOTTO

1.2 kg. boneless lamb roast
1 tablespoon cooking oil
625 ml. vegetable juice
200 grams brown rice
2 teaspoons curry powder
¼ teaspoon salt
2 medium carrots, diced
1 medium green pepper, diced

Trim any fat from the roast. In a large frying pan brown roast on all sides in the hot oil. In a slow cooker, combine juice, uncooked rice, curry powder and salt. Add the carrots and place the roast on top. Cover and cook on low heat for 8 to 9 hours. Add the green pepper to cooker. Cover and let stand 5-10 minutes. Serves 6.

EASY LAMB SHANKS

8 lamb shanks
800 grams canned tomatoes
12 baby potatoes
2 carrots, sliced
300 grams canned butter beans, drained
250 ml. red wine
40 grams French onion soup mix
chopped parsley, to serve

Combine all ingredients in slow cooker insert. Cook for 10 hours on medium setting. Sprinkle with parsley to serve. Serves 4-6.

GERMAN LAMB IN SOUR CREAM

900 grams lean boneless lamb cut into 1 inch cubes
2 tablespoons vegetable oil
227 grams flour
2 teaspoon salt
½ teaspoon dill seed
½ teaspoon caraway seed
¼ teaspoon leaf rosemary
1 large onion -- chopped
375 ml. beef broth
1 teaspoon tarragon vinegar
2 teaspoons flour
2 teaspoons water
250 ml. sour cream

Brown the lamb in oil in a frying pan. Drain well. Combine the first measure of flour with the salt, dill seed, caraway seed and rosemary. Toss the lamb cubes in the mixture to coat thoroughly. Place the lamb cubes in a lightly oiled slow cooker. Stir in all the remaining ingredients except the second measure of flour, the water and the sour cream; cover. Cook on the low setting for 10 to 14 hours. Turn to high 30 minutes before serving. Combine the second measure of flour with the water. Stir into the slow cooker. Cover. Cook until thickened. Stir in the sour cream. Serve over hot buttered noodles and garnish with additional sour cream. Serves 4.

GREEK LAMB VEGETABLES AND FETA CHEESE

450 grams lean lamb cut into bite size pieces
4 small yellow crookneck squash cut into ¼ inch thick slices
1 small red bell pepper, cut into 1 inch cubes
60 grams feta cheese, diced
1 teaspoon dried oregano leaves
½ teaspoon garlic powder
1 teaspoon salt optional
¼ teaspoon ground black pepper
4 teaspoons fresh lemon juice
65 ml. water
4 lemon wedges

Cut 4 sheets of foil, about 18 x 11 inches each. Place the foil, shiny side down, on work surface. Spray an area about the size of a salad plate in center of each piece with nonstick olive oil spray. Top each foil piece with ¼ of the lamb, then with ¼ of the squash, then ¼ of the green onions, bell pepper and feta cheese. Sprinkle each portion with ¼ of the oregano leaves, garlic powder, salt and black pepper. Drizzle each with 1 teaspoon lemon juice. Bring short sides of foil together. Fold over twice. Fold sides up twice to seal. Place in a 4 quart slow cooker with folded side up. Pour water around packets. Cover and cook on low setting for 6-7 hours or until lamb is tender. To serve, place each sealed packet on a dinner plate. Garnish each with a wedge of lemon. Serves 4.

FRENCH ONION LAMB AU JUS

lamb leg, rolled
garlic clove; crushed
1 ¼ litres water
125 ml. cup soy sauce
1 packet onion soup mix
2 onions, large sweet; sliced

Combine all ingredients in a slow cooker. Cook for 8 to 10 hours on low setting. Remove roast and allow to stand for 20 minutes before carving. Slice thin. Make sandwiches using French rolls or large croissants, sliced and buttered with slices of Swiss cheese. Dip in bowls of the onion soup broth. Also can be made into a complete dinner by adding vegetables to the broth.

HONEYED LAMB

3 tablespoons butter
1 x 2 kg. leg of lamb
salt and pepper
1 tablespoon cornflour, for thickening
1/8 teaspoon ground ginger
300 ml dry cider
4 tablespoons clear honey
1 tablespoon rosemary

Preheat crockpot on high. Heat butter in large frying pan and brown lamb on all sides. Season with salt and pepper. Transfer to crockpot. Stir the cornflour and ginger into the butter, mixing well. Add cider and honey and bring to the boil, stirring continuously. Pour the mixture over the lamb. Sprinkle with rosemary. Cook on high setting for 5-7 hours or until cooked through, depending on your crockpot. Baste once or twice during cooking. Serves 8.

IRISH STEW

900 grams boneless lamb, cubed, browned and drained
2 teaspoons salt
¼ teaspoon pepper
500 ml. water
1 small bay leaf
2 medium carrots, pared and cut into ½ inch slices
2 small onions, thinly sliced
4 medium potatoes, pared and quartered
¼ cup quick-cooking tapioca (optional)
250 grams frozen peas or 250 grams frozen mixed vegetables

Season cubed lamb with salt and pepper. Add remaining ingredients except peas (omit tapioca if you don't want gravy thickened). Stir well. Cover and cook on low setting for 10-12 hours. Add peas during last 1-2 hours of cooking.

JAMAICAN CURRIED LAMB

2 tablespoons cooking oil
680 grams boneless lamb, cut in 1 inch cubes
2 large onions, peeled and finely sliced
2 teaspoons ground mixed spice
365 ml. stock or bouillon
1 tablespoon wine or cider vinegar
1 teaspoon (or more) curry powder
salt to taste
1/8 teaspoon cayenne pepper
1 whole habanera pepper, cut top off and discard seeds

Sear lamb cubes in a frying pan over medium-high heat. Remove lamb; cook onion in oil until soft but not brown. Transfer to the crockpot; add remaining ingredients, stirring to combine. Cover and cook on low setting for 8 to 10 hours. Discard habanera pepper before serving. Serves 4.

LAMB AND APPLE CASSEROLE

900 grams middle neck lamb chops
salt and pepper
2 medium onions
2 medium carrots
1 cooking apple
30 grams plain flour
2 tablespoons oil
350 ml. stock
1 stick celery

Coat the chops with the flour seasoned with the pepper and salt. Brown on both sides in the oil and remove the chops. Cook the chopped onions in the oil until soft and golden and put into the slow cooker. Work any remaining flour into the fat, cook for 2 minutes, and stir in the stock. Bring to the boil, stirring well. Put the thinly-sliced carrots, celery and apple into the slow cooker. Put the chops on top and pour over the thickened stock, seasoning to taste. Cover and cook on high setting for 30 minutes, then on low setting for 6-7 hours.

LAMB AND VEGETABLE STEW

900 grams stewing lamb
2 tomatoes
1 summer squash
1 zucchini
1 potato
1 can mushrooms, sliced
½ bell pepper, chopped
1 large onion, chopped
2 teaspoons salt
1 clove garlic, crushed
½ teaspoon thyme leaves
1 bay leaf
500 ml. chicken stock
2 tablespoons butter
2 tablespoons flour

Peel, seed, and chop tomatoes. Slice summer squash and zucchini. Dice potatoes. Place lamb and vegetables in crockpot. Mix salt, garlic, thyme, and bay leaf into stock; pour over lamb and vegetables. Cover and cook on low setting for 8 hours. (Don't peek, lifting the lid prolongs cooking time!) Turn to high setting. Blend flour and butter, then shape into small balls. Drop into stew and cook, stirring several times, until thickened. Serve over hot noodles or rice. Serves 6-8.

LAMB CHOPS

1 tablespoon vegetable oil
4 loin lamb chops
2 tablespoons all-purpose flour
350 ml. beef broth or chicken broth
1 can diced tomatoes
1 clove of garlic, crushed
1 scant tablespoon tomato paste
4 ribs celery, thinly sliced
1 teaspoon salt
freshly-ground pepper to taste
chopped parsley

Heat oil in pan. Coat lamb chops with flour and brown quickly. Transfer chops to slow cooker. Add remaining ingredients to pan and bring to the boil. Pour over lamb and cook on setting for 30 minutes, then on low setting for 5-7 hours. Taste to check seasoning and sprinkle with plenty of chopped parsley. Serves 4.

LAMB-STUFFED GREEN PEPPERS

6 medium green peppers
450 grams lean minced lamb
1 medium onion, chopped
2 tablespoons light olive oil
300 grams cooked rice, preferably Basmati
½ teaspoon salt
¼ teaspoon pepper
¼ teaspoon oregano
¼ teaspoon cumin
250 ml. beef broth
2 teaspoons cornflour
3 tablespoons tomato paste
1 teaspoon fresh lemon juice
125 ml. sour cream

Cut the tops off the peppers, remove seeds and fibre. Brown the lamb and onion in the oil. Mix in rice and the seasonings. Fill the peppers with this mixture. Put pepper tops in the bottom of crockpot and place the peppers on top. Pour in the broth. Cover and cook on low setting for 6 hours. Remove peppers. Mix in cornflour, tomato paste, lemon juice and sour cream with the remaining broth. Return peppers to cooker, cover and cook on high setting for 30 minutes. Serve the sauce with the peppers. Serves 6.

LAMB CHOPS WITH ORANGE

8 lamb rib chops
2 tablespoons vegetable oil
½ cup orange juice
2 tablespoons honey
1 teaspoon salt
2 tablespoons cornflour
¼ teaspoon thyme
1 teaspoon grated orange peel

Heat oil in a heavy frying pan over medium heat, brown lamb chops on both sides; drain well. Whisk together the orange juice, honey, salt, cornflour, thyme, and grated orange peel. Place browned lamb chops in crockpot; pour in orange mixture, turning chops to coat well. Cover and cook on low setting for 7 to 9 hours (high setting for 3½ to 4½ hours). Serves 4 to 8.

LAMB HOT POT

1 tablespoon canola oil
4 loin lamb chops
2 tablespoons plain flour
200 ml. chicken or beef broth
14 ounces canned tomatoes
1 garlic clove, crushed
2 teaspoons tomato paste
4 celery stalks, thinly sliced
1 teaspoon salt
freshly-ground pepper to taste
chopped parsley

Heat oil in pan. Coat chops with flour and brown quickly. Transfer to slow cooker. Add remaining ingredients to pan and bring to the boil. Pour over lamb and cook on high setting for 30 minutes, then on low setting for 5 to 7 hours. Taste to check seasoning and sprinkle with plenty of chopped parsley. This recipe yields 4 servings.

LAMB SHANKS, SAUSAGES AND BEANS

225 grams chopped onion
3 tablespoons butter
450 grams small white beans, soaked overnight, drained
3 lamb shanks
4 carrots, sliced
salt and pepper, to taste
1 bay leaf
4 mild Italian sausages, cooked and sliced ½ - inch thick

Cook beans in boiling water for 30 minutes; drain. Place beans in bottom of slow cooker; add remaining ingredients except sausages, with 6 cups hot water. Cover and cook on high setting for 1 hour, then on low setting for 8 to 10 hours. Add sausages, cover and cook on high 30 minutes.

LAMB STEW

1.4 kg. boneless lamb, cut in cubes
40 grams flour
2 teaspoons salt
¼ teaspoon flour
65 ml. olive oil
500 ml. water
225 grams Bisto
1 green pepper, coarsely chopped
½ teaspoon marjoram
3 garlic cloves, crushed
2 medium potatoes, peeled and cubed
2 medium onions, chopped
1 stick celery, sliced
5 carrots, sliced

In a resealable bag, mix together the flour, seasoned salt and seasoned pepper. Add lamb and shake to coat. In a large frying pan add olive oil and brown the lamb cubes. Remove and place in crockpot. In a medium bowl, whisk together the water, gravy mix, marjoram and garlic. Add the vegetables and gravy liquid to crockpot and mix well. Cover and cook on low setting for 8-10 hours. Serves 4-6.

LAMB WITH BALSAMIC-GLAZED VEGETABLES

1 teaspoon salt
1 teaspoon fresh ground black pepper
1 teaspoon ground coriander
2 teaspoons dried rosemary leaves
1 teaspoon dried mint
1 teaspoon dried thyme
1 teaspoon ground fennel
1 large red onion, cut into eighths
1.25 kilos boneless lamb roast, well trimmed of fat
2 medium zucchini, bias-cut into ½ inch slices
2 crookneck yellow squash, bias-cut into ½ inch slices
2 medium new potatoes, quartered
3 tablespoons balsamic vinegar

Combine seasonings in a small bowl. Rub seasonings all over lamb roast. Place onion in the bottom of the crockpot. Place lamb roast on top of onion, then add remaining vegetables. Drizzle balsamic vinegar over the vegetables. Cover and cook on high setting for 1 hour, then turn to low for 10 to 12 hours. Serves 6-8.

LEG OF LAMB

1 leg of lamb to fit your slow cooker, or cut to fit
salt and pepper
a knob of butter or margarine
garlic, optional

Cut off ALL the fat and put the leg in the crockpot. Sprinkle with pepper and a knob of butter or margarine. Cook for 8 to 10 hours on low setting. When cooked drain the liquid residue into a couple of mugs, cover with foil, freeze for about half an hour or until the fat has solidified. Lift the fat off and add the remaining stock to the gravy.

LOW FAT BALTI LAMB CURRY

olive oil flavoured cooking spray
800 grams lamb, trimmed of all fat and cubed
1 brown onion, finely chopped
2 garlic cloves, crushed
125 ml. Balti curry paste
250 ml. vegetable stock (or chicken)
1 x 400 gram can tomatoes, crushed
100 grams baby spinach
coriander leaves, to serve

Heat pan over medium heat, add 1/3 of the lamb and using olive oil spray, cook for 3-5 minutes or until browned, then transfer to plate and repeat with remaining lamb in two batches, spraying more oil if required. Sauté onions, cook stirring for 2 minutes or until onion is soft, then add garlic and curry paste, cook stirring for 3 minutes. Gradually stir in stock and tomatoes, return lamb and any juices to pan, bring to boil, reduce heat to medium low, cover and simmer, stirring occasionally for 1 hour. Remove lid, simmer uncovered, stirring occasionally for 30 minutes or until lamb is tender and sauce reduced and thickened slightly. Remove from heat, stir in spinach, cover and stand for 1 minute or until spinach just wilted. Serve with rice in bowls, spoon over lamb curry and sprinkle with coriander and serve. Serves 4.

MARINATED LAMB

900 grams boneless lamb, cut in 2-inch pieces
1½ finely-chopped onions
1 cup chopped tomatoes
1½ tablespoons peeled and minced ginger
1 tablespoon minced garlic
1 tablespoon coriander powder
1½ teaspoons cumin powder
¾ teaspoon cayenne
¾ teaspoon turmeric
Salt to taste
2 chopped green chilies
1 cup plain non-fat yogurt, stirred smooth at room temperature
1 teaspoon Corn flour stirred into yogurt
2 tablespoons oil
2/3 cup chopped cilantro (divided use)
1 teaspoon gram masala

In a large saucepan, combine all ingredients except 1/3 cup of cilantro and gram masala. Mix well and let marinate 30 minutes. Cover saucepan and bring to the boil. Transfer to slow cooker, and cook on low setting for 5 to 7 hours until meat is fork-tender. If too much liquid remains after meat is cooked, remove cover, raise heat, and reduce until gravy is thick. Turn off heat, sprinkle with garam masala (or mixture of ¼ teaspoon each of ground cinnamon, ground cardamom, ground clove, and pepper), cover and let rest 5 minutes. Garnish with remaining cilantro, and serve in bowls over white rice or an Indian bread. Makes 8 servings.

MOROCCAN LAMB AND RICE

450 grams boneless lamb, cut into 1 inch pieces
1 small apple, shredded
1 packet rice and vermicelli mix with chicken seasoning
375 ml. chicken broth
1 teaspoon curry powder
50 grams raisins
50 grams slivered almonds

In a large slow cooker, combine lamb, apple, seasoning packet from rice mix, broth and curry powder; mix well. Cover and cook on low setting for 7 to 9 hours. About 25 minutes before serving, add rice and raisins; mix well. Cover; cook on high setting for an additional 20 minutes or until rice is tender. Garnish with almonds.

PERSIAN LAMB STEW

680 grams lean boneless leg of lamb, cut into 1 inch cubes
½ teaspoon salt
pepper
3 tablespoons olive oil (divided)
2 large onions, thinly sliced
6 cloves garlic, minced
½ teaspoon dried oregano
1 can whole tomatoes, drained
1 large potato, peeled and cut into ½ inch cubes
225 grams fresh green beans
1 small eggplant, peeled and cut into ½ inch cubes
1 medium zucchini, cut into ½ inch slices
5 bay leaves
3 tablespoons fresh parsley, chopped

Season the lamb with about half of the salt and pepper. In a frying pan over medium-high heat. Brown the lamb in 2 tablespoons of olive oil and transfer the lamb to a large crockpot. Sauté the onions in the last tablespoon of oil for about 3 to 5 munites until they are translucent. Add the garlic and oregano, cook and stir for approximately 1 minute. Add tomatoes and simmer, mashing the tomatoes as you stir. Pour about half of the tomatoes over the lamb in the crockpot. Place potatoes in a layer on top of the tomatoes and season with salt and pepper. Add a layer of green beans, then the eggplant and zucchini. Season each layer lightly with salt and pepper to your taste. Pour remaining tomatoes on top. Add bay leaves. Cover and cook on high for 4 hours or until the lamb is tender. Remove bay leaves and serve. Serves 4-6.

ROAST LAMB

1.8 kgs. lamb roast (or venison)
2 tablespoons flour
oil
2 cloves garlic, crushed
1 large onion, sliced
2 tablespoons brown sugar
1 tablespoon Worcestershire sauce
1 teaspoon mustard
125 ml. vinegar or lemon juice
1 x 454 gram can tomatoes

Dredge lamb with flour and brown in oil. Place in slow cooker. Add remaining ingredients. Cover and cook on high setting for 2 hours, then turn to low setting for 8-10 hours.

ROSEMARY LAMB CHILLI

450 grams lamb chops or stewing lamb, trimmed and cubed
1 large onion, chopped
2 garlic cloves
1 can diced tomatoes (do not drain)
1 can white kidney beans (do not drain)
1 can red kidney beans (do not drain)
1 tablespoon lemon juice
1 teaspoon sugar
ground pepper, to taste
salt, to taste
2 tablespoons dried rosemary
feta cheese (optional)

Brown lamb, onion, and garlic in a non-stick frying pan. Place meat mixture and the rest of the ingredients except for cheese in a slow cooker. Cover and cook on low setting for 6 hours or more, depending on how thick you like it. Serve hot, sprinkled with feta cheese. Serves 4.

PORK

APPLE GLAZED PORK ROAST

1.8 kg. pork loin roast
6 apples
60 ml. apple juice
3 tablespoons brown sugar
1 teaspoon ground ginger

Rub roast with salt and pepper. Brown pork roast, and drain well. Core and quarter apples. Place apple quarters in bottom of crockpot. Place roast on top of apples. Combine apple juice, brown sugar, and ginger. Spoon over top surface of roast, moistening well. Cover and cook on low setting for 10-12 hours, until done.

AUTUMN PORK CHOPS

6 pork chops
2 medium acorn squash, unpeeled
¾ teaspoon salt
2 tablespoons melted butter
135 grams brown sugar
¾ teaspoon brown sauce
1 tablespoon orange juice
½ teaspoon grated orange peel

Trim excess fat from chops. Cut each squash into 4 to 5 crosswise slices and remove seeds. Arrange 3 chops on bottom of crockpot. Place all squash slices on top, then another layer of the remaining 3 chops. Combine salt, butter, sugar, brown sauce, orange juice, and orange peel. Spoon over chops. Cover and cook on low setting for 4 to 6 hours or until done. Serve one or two slices of squash with each pork chop. Serves 6.

AUTUMN PORK ROAST

1.8 kg. pork roast
salt & pepper
225 grams cranberries, finely chopped
60 ml. honey
1 teaspoon grated orange peel
1/8 teaspoon ground cloves
1/8 teaspoon ground nutmeg

Sprinkle roast with salt and pepper. Place in crockpot. Combine remaining ingredients. Pour over roast. Cover, and cook on low setting for 8 to 10 hours. or on high setting for 4-5 .Makes 6 to 8 servings.

BACON CHEESE DIP

16 slices bacon, diced, fried and drained
450 grams cream cheese, softened and cubed
400 grams grated cheddar cheese
250 ml. single cream
2 teaspoons Worcestershire sauce
1 teaspoon dried minced onion
½ teaspoon dry mustard
½ teaspoon salt
dash hot sauce

Put all ingredients in the crockpot and cook on low setting for about an hour, stirring occasionally until cheese melts. Taste and adjust seasonings, add bacon, and keep on low to serve. Serve with cubed or sliced French bread.

BAKED HAM IN FOIL

Pour 120 ml. water in Crockpot. Wrap precooked 1.4 kg. to 1.8 kg. ham in foil, and place in crockpot. Cover and cook on high setting for 1 hour, then on low setting for 6 to 7 hours or until ham is hot. If cooking a larger ham, cook 1 hour on high then on low for 8 to 10 hours.

BARBECUE PORK ROAST

1 pork roast (or beef)
juice of 1 lemon
1 small onion, cut up
1 teaspoon sugar
1 bottle barbecue sauce

Cook roast covered in water (start with hot water) in crockpot overnight on low setting for 10 to 12 hours. Pour off water and pull meat into grated pieces. Sauté onion in a little butter. Combine barbecue sauce, onions, sugar and juice of lemon with meat in crockpot and cook on high setting for 1½ to 2½ hours, or on low setting for 3 to 6 hours.

BARBECUE PORK SANDWICHES

1 pork roast
1 bottle barbecue sauce
250 ml. water

Just throw the pork into the crockpot and cook on high setting for about 6 hours or low setting for about 10 hours. When it's done, just remove meat from bone and serve on hamburger buns or rolls with more barbecue sauce or ketchup, etc.

BARBECUED PORK STRIPS

120 ml. soy sauce
60 ml. dry sherry
100 grams brown sugar
2 cloves garlic, crushed
1/8 teaspoon pepper
120 ml. barbecue sauce
1 can pineapple chunks (do not drain)
1.5 kg. lean pork, cut into strips, browned, and drained

Combine all ingredients except pork strips in crockpot and stir well. Add pork and stir to coat. Cook on low setting , covered, for 8 to 10 hours. Serve with sauce. Makes about 15 servings.

BEST PORK ROAST

1 x 225 kg. pork roast
6-8 cloves garlic
pepper
basil
250 ml. dry white wine
onion

Cut 6 to 8 holes into the roast just big enough to fit a clove of garlic. Put a peeled garlic clove into each hole. Rub outside with cracked pepper and basil. Pour dry white wine into the bottom of the crockpot. Place roast in the crockpot, and put slices or wedges of onion on top and around the roast. Cover and cook on low setting all day or until cooked.

BLACK BEAN CHILLI WITH PORK

450 grams. boneless pork, cut into cubes
2 x (450 grams.) cans black beans, drained
1 red or yellow bell pepper, chopped
1 medium tomato, peeled, seeded and chopped
1 small red onion, thinly sliced
1 clove garlic, crushed
½ teaspoon ground cumin
2 teaspoons chilli powder
½ teaspoon salt
1 can tomato sauce
115 grams sour cream
2 tablespoons chopped cilantro

In a crockpot, stir together pork, beans, bell pepper, tomato, onion, garlic, cumin, chilli powder, salt, and tomato sauce. Cover and cook on low setting for 8 to 9 hours. Spoon into bowls and top with sour cream and cilantro.

BRACIOLE

230 grams Italian sausage
1 kg. stead, cut ¼ to ½ inch thick
1 tablespoon dried parsley flakes
½ teaspoon leaf oregano
2 cloves garlic, crushed
1 large onion, finely chopped
1 teaspoon salt
1 can Italian style tomatoes
1 x 170 gram can tomato paste
1 teaspoon salt
1 teaspoon leaf oregano
10 large tomatoes
8 cloves galic, chopped
1 tablespoon Worcestershire sauce
2 teaspoons salt
2 large onions, chopped
1 tablespon flour
1 tablespoon vegetable oil
1 teaspoon oregano
1 teaspoon thyme
1 tablespoon wine vinegar
1 tablespoon sugar

Trim all excess fat from steak. Cut into 8 evenly-shaped pieces. Pound steak pieces between greaseproof paper until very thin and easy to roll. In frying pan, lightly brown sausage. Drain well and combine with parsley, ½ teaspoon oregano, garlic, onion and salt; mix well. Spread each steak with 2 to 3 tablespoons of sausage mixture. Roll up steaks and tie. Stack steak rolls in crockpot. Combine tomatoes, tomato paste, salt and 1 teaspoon oregano; pour over rolls cook and cover on low setting for 8 to 10 hours. Serve steak rolls with sauce.

SAUCE Place all ingredients except flour, oil and vinegar in crockpot; stir well. Cover and cook on low setting for 8 to 10 hours. Remove cover and turn to high setting for the last hour to reduce excess moisture. Before removing sauce from crockpot, stir in flour, oil and vinegar. Allow to cool. Four 600 grams of sauce at a time into blender container, blend until smooth.

CAJUN BREW PORK N BEANS

5 cans pork-n-beans (2nd to smallest size)
2 230 grams cans tomato sauce
2 onions (chopped)
1/4 bottle barbeque sauce
the following are "to taste"
Worcestershire sauce
hot sauce
Cajun seasoning
liquid smoke
mustard
brown sugar

Mix all ingredients in a crockpot and crank it up to high. Let it cook all day, stirring occasionally. Can also be made on the stove top, but let it simmer for several hours stirring occasionally.

CAJUN SAUSAGE & RICE

230 grams sausage, cut in ¼ inch slices
1 x 410 gram can diced tomatoes with liquid
1 medium onion, diced
1 medium green pepper, diced
2 celery stalks, thinly sliced
1 tablespoon chicken stock granules
1 tablespoon steak sauce
3 bay leaves or 1 teaspoon dried thyme
1 teaspoon sugar
¼ to ½ teaspoon hot pepper sauce
225 grams uncooked instant rice
120 grams chopped parsley (optional)

Combine sausage, tomatoes, onion, green pepper, celery stock, steak sauce, bay leaves, sugar and hot pepper sauce in crockpot. Cover and cook on low setting for 8 hours. Remove the bay leaves; stir in rice and 120 ml. of water. Cook an additional 25 minutes. Stir in parsley if desired. Makes 5 servings

CANNELLONI ALLA CATANIA

450 grams dried cannellini beans (white kidney beans)
1.5 litres water
2 hot Italian sausages, sliced
1 large onion, chopped
1 large garlic clove, crushed
2 large tomatoes, ripe, peeled and coarsely chopped
1 bay leaf, crumbled
½ teaspoon thyme, crumbled
½ teaspoon basil, crumbled
3 x 1 inch strips of orange rind
1 teaspoon salt
¼ teaspoon pepper
1 beef OXO cube

Pick over beans and rinse. Cover beans with water in a large saucepan. Bring to the boil, cover. Cook 2 minutes, remove from heat, and allow to stand for 1 hour. Pour into slow cooker. Brown sausages in a small frying pan, and set aside. Sauté onion and garlic in the same pan until soft, then stir in tomato, bay leaf, thyme, basil, orange strips, salt and pepper and instant beef broth. Bring to the boil. Stir into beans. Cover and cook on low setting for 10 hours or on high for 5 hours or until beans are tender. Serves 6.

CANTONESE DINNER

675 grams pork steak ½ inch thick, cut into strips
2 tablespoons oil
1 large onion, sliced
1 small green pepper, cut into strips
1 can mushrooms, drained
1 x 225 gram can tomato sauce
3 tablespoons brown sugar
1½ tablespoon vinegar
1½ teaspoon salt
2 teaspoons Worcestershire sauce

Brown pork in oil in a frying pan. Drain on a double paper towel. Place pork strips and all remaining ingredients into a crockpot. Cover and cook on low setting for 6 to 8 hours or on high for 4 hours. Serve over hot fluffy rice.

CANTONESE PORK DINNER

900 grams pork steaks
2 tablespoons vegetable oil
1 onion, thinly sliced
1 x 130 gram can mushrooms, drained
1 x 230 gram can tomato sauce
3 tablespoons brown sugar
1½ teaspoons distilled white vinegar
1½ teaspoons salt
2 tablespoons Worcestershire sauce

In a heavy frying pan heat oil over medium high heat. Add pork strips and brown. Drain off excess fat. Place meat, onion, mushrooms, tomato sauce, brown sugar, vinegar, salt, and Worcestershire sauce in a slow cooker. Cook on high setting for 4 hours, or on low for 6 to 8 hours. Serve hot.

CASSEROLE IN THE COOKER

450 grams broccoli, thawed and drained
600 grams cubed fully-cooked ham
1 can condensed cream of mushroom soup, undiluted
225 grams processed cheese sauce
250 ml. milk
200 grams uncooked instant rice
1 celery rib, chopped
1 small onion, chopped

In a slow cooker, combine broccoli and ham. Combine the soup, cheese sauce, milk, rice, celery and onion; stir into the broccoli mixture. Cover and cook on low setting for 4-5 hours or until rice is tender. 4 servings.

CHEESY BACON DIP

500 grams cream cheese, softened and cut into cubes
400 grams grated cheese
250 ml. single cream
2 tablespoons mustard
1 tablespoon chopped onion
2 teaspoon Worcestershire sauce
½ teaspoon salt
¼ teaspoon hot pepper sauce
450 grams bacon, cooked and crumbled

Place cream cheese, cheese, single cream, mustard, onion,
Worcestershire sauce, salt and pepper sauce in crockpot. Cover and cook on low setting (stirring occasionally) for one hour, or until cheese melts. Stir in bacon, and adjust the seasonings. Serve with crusty bread or crackers.

CROCKPOT CHICKEN FRIED CHOPS

55 grams flour
2 teaspoon salt
1 ½ teaspoon ground mustard
½ teaspoon garlic powder
6 pork chops, trimmed
2 tablespoons vegetable oil
1 can cream of chicken soup, undiluted
80 ml. water

In a shallow bowl, combine flour, salt, mustard and garlic powder; dredge pork chops. In a frying pan, brown the chops on both sides in oil. Place in a slow cooker. Combine soup and water, and pour over chops. Cover and cook on low setting for 6 to 8 hours or until meat is tender. If desired, thicken pan juices and serve with the pork chops.

BEST DIP EVER

1 packet cream cheese
1 can chilli (no beans)
450 grams medium or spicy sausage, browned and crumbled

Cook in crockpot on low setting and cook until the cheese melts.

CHOPS IN A CROCK

6 pork chops, browned
1 onion, chopped
3 tablespoons ketchup
300 grams can cream of mushroom soup
2 teaspoons Worcestershire sauce

Place into crockpot and cook on low setting for about 4 to 5 hours. Serve with rice, noodles or potatoes.

CHOPS OR RIBS

6 or 8 chops or ribs to fill crockpot
60 grams chopped onion
115 grams chopped celery
250 ml. ketchup
125 ml. water
65 ml. lemon juice
2 tablespoon brown sugar
3 tablespoon Worcestershire sauce
2 tablespoon vinegar
1 tablespoon mustard
½ teaspoon salt
¼ teaspoon pepper

Mix together and pour over meat in pot. Cook until tender.

COLA BARBECUE PORK ROAST

1 pork roast
375 ml. cola
1 bottle barbecue sauce

Cut all visible fat from roast, put in crockpot and cook on low setting for 12 hours. Remove meat from crockpot and drain off juice. Shred meat and return to crockpot. Add 1 bottle of barbecue sauce and cook for a further 5 to 6 hours. Makes a lot!

COLA HAM

100 grams brown sugar
1 teaspoon dry mustard
60 ml. cola (Coca Cola®, Pepsi Cola®, etc)
1.8 kilos pre-cooked ham

Combine brown sugar and mustard. Moisten with cola to make a smooth paste. Reserve remaining cola. Score the ham with shallow slashes in a diamond pattern. Rub ham with mixture. Place ham in crockpot and add remaining cola. Cover and cook on high setting for 1 hour, then turn to low setting and cook for 6 to 7 hours. Serves 9 to 12.

CORNY HAM AND POTATO SCALLOP

5 potatoes, peeled and cubed
1.2 kilos cubed cooked ham
1 x (425 gram) can whole kernel corn, drained
60 grams chopped green bell pepper
2 teaspoons instant minced onion
1 can condensed cheddar cheese soup
120 ml. milk
3 tablespoons plain flour

In a slow cooker, combine potatoes, ham, corn, green pepper and onion; mix well. In a small bowl, combine soup, milk and flour; beat with wire whisk until smooth. Pour soup mixture over potato mixture and stir gently to mix. Cover and cook on low setting for about 8 hours or until potatoes are tender.

CRANBERRY PORK

1 x 450 gram can cranberry sauce
80 ml. French salad dressing
1 onion, sliced
1.5 kg. pork roast

In a medium bowl, combine the cranberry sauce, salad dressing and onions. Place pork in a slow cooker and pour the sauce over the pork. Cook on high setting for 4 hours or on low setting for 8 hours. Pork is cooked when its internal temperature has reached 160°F (70°C).

CRANBERRY PORK ROAST

4 medium potatoes, peeled and cut into 1 inch cubes
1 x 1.75 gram boneless pork loin roast, rolled and tied
1 can (450 grams) whole-berry cranberry sauce
1 can apricot nectar
1 medium onion, coarsely chopped
75 grams coarsely chopped dried apricots
100 grams sugar
1 teaspoon dry mustard
1/4 teaspoon crushed red pepper

Place the potatoes in a large slow cooker, then place the roast over the potatoes. In a large bowl, combine the remaining ingredients; mix well and pour over the roast. Cover and cook on low setting for 5 to 6 hours. Remove the roast to a cutting board and thinly slice. Serve with the potatoes and sauce. Serves 4 to 6.

CRAZY STANDING UP PORK CHOPS

4 loin pork chops (lean)
2 medium onions, sliced
1 teaspoon butter
salt and pepper, to taste
spices of your choice

Stand chops in crockpot, thin side down. Sprinkle with salt, pepper and spices of your choice. Cover with the onion slices, which have been separated into rings. Place butter on top, and cook on low setting for 6 to 8 hours, or until chops are tender and onions are cooked. The result is moist, tender chops with a deep brown colour as if baked in the oven. Serves 4.

CROCKED SAUSAGES

230 grams lean minced beef
450 grams sausage, sliced
1 x 225 gram can whole tomatoes (do not drain)
255 grams frozen french-cut green beans
1 x 170 gram can pitted black olives, drained and left whole
120 ml. red wine
3 garlic cloves, crushed
1 medium onion, sliced
1 medium green pepper, chopped
1 teaspoon basil, crushed
1 teaspoon oregano, crushed
½ teaspoon thyme, crushed
¼ teaspoon pepper
450 grams pasta of your choice
115 grams freshly-grated parmesan

In a medium frying pan, sauté minced beef. When browned, transfer to crockpot. Add all other ingredients except pasta and parmesan. Cook on low setting for 6 to 8 hours. Cook pasta according to directions. Ladle Crocked Sausages over pasta in large bowls. Garnish with the Parmesan cheese.

COUNTRY STYLE RIBS AND SAUERKRAUT

340 grams sauerkraut
brown sugar to taste
1 kilo country style ribs

Place the ribs in a crockpot. Sweeten the sauerkraut to taste with the brown sugar. Cook them all day while at work and come home to tender and delicious ribs and kraut. Mash a potato and dinner is ready!

EASY CROCKPOT PORK CHOPS

680 grams boneless pork chops
salt
pepper
115 grams thinly sliced onions
65 grams brown sugar
½ teaspoon thyme
2 x 425 gram cans stewed tomatoes (do not drain)

Lightly salt and pepper both sides of the pork chops and place them into the crockpot. Top with sliced onion, then brown sugar and thyme. Pour the undrained stewed tomatoes over top. Cover and cook on low setting for 6 to 8 hours. Serves 4 to 6.

LEFTOVER PORK ROAST CASSEROLE

1 packet cooked noodles
1 packet beans (any type is fine)
beef stock
1 packet long grain rice
3 potatoes, cut into 1 inch cubes
leftover pork from your roast
salt and pepper to taste

Fill your crockpot a little more than half way with water, then flavour it with the beef stock to taste. Add the sliced up potatoes, beans and rice. Cook until potatoes and rice are done (most of the day on low setting or half a day on high setting). Add the pork and let that cook while you boil the noodles. Add the noodles to the pot when they're cooked. Cook for a further 5 to 10 more minutes and serve.

HOT DIP

450 grams Italian sausage - hot
450 grams cheese
1 can tomatoes (drained)
1 jar hot piquant sauce
1 jalapeno pepper, finely diced

Brown sausage and drain along with jalapeno pepper. Add to slow cooker with other ingredients and cook on low setting for one hour or more until melted and blended. Serve with tortilla strips or chips, large Doritos corn chips, or even lightly toasted and cubed bread.

PORK, APPLE AND CRANBERRY STEW

800 grams boneless pork roast
salt and pepper to taste
450 grams Granny Smith apples, thinly sliced
120 grams sweet onions, thinly sliced
120 grams cranberries
250 ml. apple cider or apple juice
250 ml. chicken broth
3 tablespoons brown sugar
½ teaspoon dried rubbed sage

Season pork roast with salt and pepper. Brown on all sides in a frying pan. Meanwhile, put a layer of apples on the bottom of the crockpot. When the meat is browned, place it on top of the apples. Add the rest of the apples, the onion, and the cranberries around and on top of the pork. Mix the apple cider, the chicken broth, the brown sugar and the sage. Pour over the pork and fruit. Cover and cook on high setting for 6 to 7 hours until the pork falls apart when you poke it with a fork. Shred the pork and mix well with the sauce. Season to taste with salt and pepper. Serve over hot buttered noodles. Serves 6 to 8.

RED RICE

4 to 6 slices bacon, fried and crumbled
1 large onion, coarsely chopped
2 cans chopped tomatoes, (425 grams each)
225 grams converted rice
225 grams cooked chopped ham
salt and pepper, to taste
1/8 teaspoon hot pepper sauce, or to taste

Fry bacon; drain and crumble. Cook onion in bacon fat just until softened. Combine all ingredients in the slow cooker. Cover and cook on low setting for 6 to 7 hours, or until rice is tender but not mushy. Serves 6 to 8

SCALLOPED POTATOES WITH HAM

120 grams diced ham
8 to 10 medium potatoes, thinly sliced
225 grams grated cheese
salt and pepper
1 can cream of mushroom soup, or 250 ml. medium white sauce
paprika
1 onion, thinly sliced

In slow cooker layer half of ham, half of potatoes, half of onions, half of cheese. Sprinkle with salt and pepper. Repeat layers with remaining half of ingredients. Spoon undiluted soup or white sauce over top and sprinkle with paprika. Cover and cook on low setting for 7 to 9 hours.

SPINACH, CHEESE & BACON STRATA

500 grams sliced and buttered French bread, cubed
1 x 450 gram bag spinach
225 grams diced, cooked bacon, ham, or turkey ham
160 grams grated cheddar cheese
salt and pepper, to taste
1 x 284 gram can cream of mushroom soup
120 ml. evaporated milk
5 eggs
1 tablespoon minced dried onion (optional)

Lightly butter a large crockpot. Layer with half of the buttered bread cubes, spinach, bacon, and cheese; salt and pepper to taste. Repeat layers ending with cheese. Whisk together the soup, milk, eggs, and dried onion. Pour over slow cooker mixture. Chill for one hour or overnight. Cover and cook on low setting for 3½ to 4½ hours. Serves 4 to 6.

SWEET AND SOUR CABBAGE

4 bacon slices, diced
60 grams packed brown sugar
2 tablespoons flour
½ teaspoon salt
1/8 teaspoon pepper
60 ml. water
60 ml. vinegar
1 medium head red cabbage, grated
1 small onion, finely chopped

In a frying pan, cook bacon until crisp; reserve fat. Combine 1 tablespoon of the fat in a slow cooker with the remaining ingredients except for the cooked bacon. Cover and cook on low setting for 6½ to 7 hours or until cabbage is tender. Spoon into serving bowl; sprinkle with reserved bacon.

SWEET AND SOUR HAM

1.5 kilos ham, cubed
6 carrots, thickly sliced
1 green pepper
½ onion
3 stalks celery
125 ml. teriyaki sauce
125 ml. chicken broth
1 teaspoon ginger, crushed
1½ teaspoons garlic salt
1 to 2 tablespoons cider vinegar
2 x cans pineapple chunks in juice (juice reserved)
15 grams cornflour

Combine all ingredients including pineapple juice, but NOT the pineapple or cornflour yet. Cook on low setting for 5 hours. Add cornflour (all of it if very liquid) and the pineapple. Cook for an additional 1 or 2 hours.   Serves 12

SWEET AND SOUR SAUSAGE BALLS

115 grams brown sugar
907 grams sausage meat
315 ml. ketchup
1 tablespoon. soy sauce
1 tablespoon. lemon juice
1 can pineapple chunks

Roll sausage meat in balls, brown and add other ingredients. Cook until done in slow cooker.

POULTRY

ARROZ CON POLLO

4 chicken breast halves, skin and excess fat removed
¼ teaspoon salt
¼ teaspoon pepper
¼ teaspoon paprika
1 tablespoon oil
1 medium onion, chopped
1 small red pepper, chopped
1 clove of garlic, crushed
½ teaspoon dried rosemary
1 large can crushed tomatoes
285 grams frozen peas

Season chicken with salt, pepper, and paprika. In a medium frying pan, heat oil over medium-high heat. Add chicken and brown. Put chicken in the crockpot. In a small bowl, combine remaining ingredients except the peas. Pour over chicken. Cover and cook on low setting for 7 to 9 hours, or on high setting for 3 to 4 hours. Add peas one hour before serving. Serve over rice. Makes 4 servings.

AUTUMN CHICKEN

2 large or 4 small chicken breasts
2 parsnips
2 carrots
1 acorn squash
1 can of chicken broth
Garlic, to taste
Salt and pepper, to taste
nutmeg
honey

Peel and chop carrots and parsnips and place them in the bottom of the crockpot. Sprinkle with garlic. Place chicken on top, and pour in broth. Cut squash into chunks and slice off the skin. Place on top of chicken. Sprinkle desired amounts of salt, pepper and nutmeg on top of squash and drizzle enough honey on top to lightly cover the squash. Cook on low setting for 8 to 10 hours.

ARTICHOKES, CHICKEN AND OLIVES

900 grams skinless, boneless chicken breast halves and/or thighs
450 grams sliced fresh mushrooms
1 large can diced tomatoes
250 grams artichokes
250 ml. chicken broth
1 medium onion, chopped
115 grams sliced pitted ripe olives (or 60 grams capers, drained)
60 grams dry white wine or chicken broth
3 tablespoon quick cooking tapioca
2 to 3 teaspoons curry powder
¾ teaspoon dried thyme, crushed
¼ teaspoon salt
¼ teaspoon pepper
500 grams hot cooked couscous

Rinse chicken and set aside. In a large crockpot combine mushrooms, un-drained tomatoes, frozen artichoke hearts, chicken broth, onion, olives, & wine/broth. Stir in tapioca, curry powder, thyme, salt, & pepper. Add chicken. Spoon some of the tomato mixture over chicken. Cover & cook on LOW for 7 to 8 hours or on HIGH for 3 1/2 to 4 hours. Serve with hot cooked couscous. Serves 6.

BARBECUE CHICKEN

1 chicken, cut up and skin removed
250 ml. ketchup
135 grams brown sugar
3 tablespoons Worcestershire sauce

Place chicken in crockpot. Combine remaining ingredients and pour over chicken. Cook for 4 hours on high setting or 8 to 10 hours on low. Delicious!

BOURBON BREAST OF CHICKEN

4 chicken breast halves
60 grams flour
½ teaspoon paprika
salt
2 tablespoon butter
2 tablespoons oil
2 tablespoons onion, chopped
2 tablespoons parsley, chopped
¼ teaspoon dried chervil
65 ml. bourbon
1 x 110 gram can mushrooms (do not drain)
1 x 285 gram can tomatoes
¼ teaspoon sugar
salt and pepper

Dredge chicken in flour which has been mixed with paprika and a little salt. Heat butter and oil in a frying pan and sauté chicken on both sides until lightly browned. Stir in onion, parsley and chervil and cook a moment. Remove from heat. Place chicken in slow cooker. Combine remaining ingredients and pour over chicken. Cover and cook on low setting for 6 to 7 hours. Serve with noodles or rice. Serves 4

BRAISED CHICKEN CURRY WITH YAMS

canola oil
910 grams chicken legs and thighs
2 large white onions, chopped
1 tablespoon crushed garlic
1 tablespoon crushed ginger
85 grams madras curry powder
1 banana
2 bay leaves
1.2 litres chicken stock
3 large yams (sweet potatoes), peeled and chopped
salt and black pepper to taste

In a hot saucepan coated with oil, season the chicken and brown on all sides. Place chicken in slow cooker. In the same saucepan, remove all chicken fat, leaving only a coating of oil and sauté the onions, garlic and ginger. Caramelize well, then add curry powder. Mix quickly for 2 minutes making sure not to burn the curry powder. Pour over the chicken, and add banana, bay leaves, yams and chicken stock. Check for seasonings. Cook on low setting for 4 hours. Serve on basmati rice.

BROWN RICE AND CHICKEN

225 grams diced cooked chicken
2 onions, chopped
2 stalks celery, chopped
500 grams cooked brown rice
60 ml. dry white wine
500 grams chicken broth
225 grams sliced almonds

Combine all ingredients in slow cooker. Cook on low setting for 6 to 8 hours or on automatic for 4 to 5 hours. Serve with sliced almonds lightly toasted.

BRUNSWICK STEW

1 x 1.5 kg. chicken, cut up
1.9 litres water
1 onion, chopped
1 can processed ham, cubed
3 potatoes, diced
1 x large can tomatoes, cut up
300 grams lima beans
300 grams ounces corn; whole kernel
2 teaspoons salt
1 teaspoon sugar
¼ teaspoon pepper
½ teaspoon seasoned salt

In a slow cooker combine chicken with water, onion, ham and potatoes. Cook covered on low setting for 4 to 5 hours or until chicken is cooked. Lift chicken out of pot, and remove meat from bones. Return chicken meat to slow cooker. Add tomatoes, beans, corn, salt, seasoned salt, sugar and pepper. Cover and cook on high setting for 1 hour. Makes 8 servings.

CAFE CHICKEN

1.8 kilos cut up chicken
1 onion chopped
2 (or more) cloves of garlic, (chopped, not crushed)
1 green pepper, chopped
1 medium ripe tomato, peeled and chopped
250 ml. dry white wine
pinch of cayenne pepper

Combine all ingredients in slow cooker. Coverand cook on low setting for 6 to 8 hours. If you prefer you can cook for 5½ hurs only and then place chicken on cookie sheets with sides and cook for 30-45 minutes at 350°F to crisp up the skin. Serve with crusty French bread. Serves 4-5.

CARROT CHICKEN

skinless, boneless chicken breasts
1 medium head cabbage, quartered
450 grams carrots, cut into 1 inch pieces
water to cover
4 cubes chicken stock
1 teaspoon poultry seasoning
¼ teaspoon Greek-style seasoning
2 tablespoons cornflour
60 ml. water

Rinse chicken and place in slow cooker. Rinse cabbage and place on top of chicken, then add carrots. Add enough water to almost cover all. Add stock cubes and sprinkle liberally with poultry seasoning. Add Greek seasoning to taste (as you would salt and pepper). Cook on low setting for 8 hours Or on high setting for 4 hours.

To Make Gravy: When you're nearly ready to eat, pour off some of the juice and place in a saucepan. Bring to the boil. Dissolve cornflour in about 60 ml. water (depending on how thick you like your gravy). Add to saucepan and simmer all together until thick. If desired, season with additional Greek seasoning. Serve gravy over chicken and potatoes, if desired.

CHEESY CHICKEN A LA TIFFANY

1 can mushroom soup
1 can cream of broccoli soup
1 can broccoli cheese soup
2 packets chicken breasts (boneless, skinless)
1 can mixed vegetables
1-2 tablespoons tapioca for thickening
125 grams grated cheddar cheese

Dice chicken put in crockpot sprinkle with salt and pepper, Pour all three cans of soup over chicken and stir. Cover and cook on low about 4-6 hours. About an hour before serving add mixed vegetables, cheese and thicken with tapioca.

CHICKEN AND NOODLES

4 carrots, sliced
4-5 pieces chicken
1 small onion, chopped
500 ml. water
4 chicken stock cubes
1 teaspoon garlic salt
salt and pepper, to taste
450 grams egg noodles

Place carrots in crockpot, followed by all ingredients except noodles. Cook on low for 8 hours. At the end of cooking time, cook egg noodles on hob. While noodles cook, remove chicken from crockpot and cut into bite-size pieces. Return chicken and noodles to crockpot. If desired, make thicken broth with cornflour and water. Just be sure to add some of the broth to your cornflour mixture first. This will prevent any lumps from forming.

CHICKEN AND DUMPLINGS

4 tablespoons butter
1 tablespoon vegetable oil
1 onion, chopped
1.5 kg. of your favourite chicken parts, cut up
500 ml. chicken broth
2 stalks celery
1 tablespoon minced parsley
2 carrots, peeled and sliced
1 teaspoon black pepper
salt to taste
½ teaspoon ground mixed spice
250 ml. dry white wine (optional but really adds a nice taste)
1 packet plain scones
120 ml. heavy cream
2 tablespoons flour

In a large frying pan, brown onion in butter and oil just until tender, then brown chicken parts and place in a large crockpot. Add remaining ingredients except heavy cream, flour and biscuits. Cook on high setting for 2½ to 3 hours, or on low setting for 5 to 7 hours. When chicken is cooked, remove pieces to a plate and allow cool, then de-bone. While chicken is cooling, mix flour and cream together, then stir into crockpot. Cut each scone into 4 pieces. Drop into crockpot and turn on high. These will need to cook about 30 minutes, until they are firm. Return chicken meat to crockpot after deboning and serve.

CHEESY CROKPOT CHICKEN

6 chicken breasts (boneless and skinless)
salt and pepper to taste
garlic granules, to taste
2 cans cream of chicken soup
1 can cheddar cheese soup

Rinse chicken and sprinkle with salt, pepper and garlic granules. Mix undiluted soup and pour over chicken in the crockpot. Cook on low setting for 6 to 8 hours. Serve over rice or noodles.

CHICKEN A LA KING

900 grams boneless chicken
200 grams matchstick-cut carrots
1 bunch green onions (scallions), sliced in ½ inch pieces
1 jar Kraft pimiento or pimiento & olive processed cheese spread
1 can cream of chicken soup
2 tablespoons dry sherry (optional)
salt and pepper to taste

Put all ingredients in a large slow cooker in the order given; stir to combine. Cover and cook on low setting for 7 to 9 hours. Serve over rice, toast, or biscuits. Serves 6 to 8.

CHICKEN AND RICE (1)

boneless, skinless chicken breast (2-1.5 kilos)
chicken flavoured rice
cream of celery soup
cream of chicken soup
250 ml. water
salt

Put rice in crockpot, add water. Combine soups and layer on top of rice. Season chicken with salt and layer chicken in pot. Cook on high setting for 4 to 5 hours or low setting for 7-10 hours.

CHICKEN AND RICE (2)

175 grams rice
1 can cream of celery soup
1 can cream of mushroom soup
1 small can whole mushrooms
1 small jar pimento strips, drained
½ green pepper, chopped
½ onion, chopped
1 can water chestnuts, drained and sliced
8 to 12 chicken breasts, halved
grated parmesan cheese

Place rice in crockpot. Combine remaining ingredients except chicken and cheese in bowl. Mix well. Pour half of mixture over rice. Place chicken on top. Pour remaining soup mixture over all. Cook on high for 3 hours or until chicken is tender. Garnish with cheese.

CHICKEN AND SAUSAGE CASSOULET

1 packet frozen lima beans
250 ml. tomato juice
1 carrot, cut into ½ inch pieces
1 stalk celery, cut into ½ inch pieces
1 onion, chopped
1 clove garlic, crushed
1 bay leaf
1 teaspoon chicken stock granules
½ teaspoon dried basil, crushed
½ teaspoon dried oregano, crushed
3 boneless chicken breasts
3 chicken drumsticks
225 grams smoked sausage

Place carrots, limas, celery and onions on bottom of crockpot which has been sprayed with cooking oil. Combine herbs, juice and stock and add to vegetables. Place chicken on top of vegetables. Cut sausage into pieces. Put chicken and sausage on top of vegetables. Cover crockpot and cook on Low setting for 10 hours or on high setting for 5 hours. Remove bay leaf before serving.

CHICKEN AND SAUSAGE PAELLA

1100 – 1350 grams meaty chicken pieces
1 tablespoon cooking oil
225 grams cooked smoked turkey sausage, halved lengthwise and sliced
1 large onion, sliced
3 cloves garlic, crushed
2 tablespoons snipped fresh thyme or 2 teaspoon dried thyme, crushed
¼ teaspoon black pepper
1/8 teaspoon thread saffron or ¼ teaspoon ground turmeric
1 x can chicken broth
240 ml. water
500 grams chopped tomatoes
2 yellow or green bell peppers, cut into very thin bite-size strips
225 grams frozen green peas
600 grams. hot cooked rice

Skin chicken, then rinse and pat dry. In a large frying pan brown chicken pieces, half at a time, in hot oil. Drain off fat. In a large crockpot place chicken pieces, turkey sausage, and onion. Sprinkle with garlic, dried thyme (if using), black pepper, and saffron or turmeric. Pour broth and water over everything. Cover and cook on low-heat setting for 7 to 8 hours or on high-heat setting for 3½ to 4 hours. Add the tomatoes, sweet peppers, peas, and if using, the fresh thyme to the cooker. Cover, and allow to stand for 5 minutes. Serve over the hot rice. Makes 6 servings.

CHICKEN CACCIATORE IN CROCKPOT

Place a cut-up chicken in slow cooker. Cover with one large un-drained can of cut-up tomatoes, one cut-up onion, one cut-up green pepper, crushed garlic (to taste), one tablespoon Italian herbs, red pepper flakes to taste. Cook on low setting for 6 to 8 hours until falling apart. Serve over pasta, sprinkling more pepper and plenty of Parmesan cheese over it!

CHICKEN CASSEROLE

1 x 250 gram packet noodles
600 grams diced cooked chicken
100 grams diced celery
100 grams diced green pepper
100 grams diced onion
1 can mushrooms
1 jar pimiento cheese spread
80 grams parmesan cheese
150 grams cream style cottage cheese
125 grams grated mature processed cheese
1 can cream of chicken soup
120 ml. chicken broth
2 tablespoons melted butter
1/2 teaspoon basil

Cook noodles according to packet directions and drain and rinse thoroughly. In a large bowl, combine remaining ingredients with noodles until well mixed. Pour mixture into greased crockpot. Cover and cook on low setting for 6 to 8 hours or high setting for 3 to 4 hours. Serves 6.

CHICKEN CHILLI

2 whole chicken breasts, skinned, de-boned, and cut in ½ inch chunks
1 celery heart
1 medium onion
2 cans stewed tomatoes, sliced
450 grams. medium salsa or piquant sauce
1 can chick peas
170 grams. mushrooms
olive oil

Brown chicken in 1 tablespoon olive oil. Chop celery, onion and mushrooms. Combine all ingredients in large crockpot, stir and simmer on low setting for 6 to 8 hours. Serve with bread or taco chips.

CHICKEN CORDON BLEU

4 to 6 chicken breasts (pounded out thin)
4 to 6 pieces of ham
4 to 6 slices of mozzarella cheese
1 can cream of mushroom soup
60 ml. milk

Put ham and cheese on chicken. Roll up and secure with a skewer. Place chicken in slow cooker so it looks like a triangle /_\ Layer the rest on top. Mix soup and milk. Pour over top of chicken. Cover and cook on low setting for 4 hours or until chicken is no longer pink. Serve over noodles with the sauce it makes.

CHICKEN ENCHILADAS

boneless, skinless chicken
1 large can enchilada sauce (green or red)
medium or large flour tortillas
grated cheese

Empty enchilada sauce into the crockpot and place chicken fillets into the sauce. Cook on low setting all day. Scoop out chicken and cut or shred onto a plate. Spread a tortilla on another plate and arrange some chicken into a "stripe" down the middle. Sprinkle liberal grated cheese, and ladle some sauce over it. Roll the tortilla up, ladle more sauce over it, and sprinkle more cheese. Place in the microwave for about 20 seconds on high setting to melt the cheese. More microwave time may be needed for multiple enchiladas on one plate.

CHICKEN IN SPICY SAUCE

120 ml. tomato juice
120 ml. soy sauce
100 grams brown sugar
60 ml. chicken broth
3 cloves garlic, crushed
1 whole chicken, cut in skinless bite- size pieces or favourite parts

Combine all ingredients except chicken in a bowl. Dip each piece of chicken in the sauce. Place in the slow cooker. Pour remaining sauce over the top. Cook on low setting for 6 to 8 hours or on high setting for 3 to 4 hours. Makes 6 servings.

CHICKEN IN A POT

1.5 kg. whole chicken, thawed
2 carrots, sliced
2 onions, sliced
2 celery stalks with leaves,
1 teaspoon basil
2 teaspoons salt
½ teaspoon black pepper
125 ml. chicken broth or wine

Put carrots, onions, and celery in bottom of crockpot. Add whole chicken. Top with salt, pepper and liquid. Sprinkle basil over top. Cover and cook until done on low setting for 8 to 10 hours. (high setting for 3 to 4 hours, using 250 ml. water). Remove chicken and vegetables with spatula.

CHICKEN NOODLE SOUP

3 carrots, peeled and cut into chunks
3 stalks celery, cut into chunks
1 large onion, quartered
3 boneless skinless chicken breast halves
2 cans chicken broth
2 to 3 soup cans of water
generous shakes of dried dill and dried parsley
225 grams. noodles

Put vegetables in crockpot. Add chicken. Pour in broth and water. Add dill and parsley. Cover and cook on low setting for 8 hours. Remove vegetables and chicken from crockpot. Add noodles, turn to high and heat while you shred the chicken and mince the vegetables.. Return chicken and vegetables to crockpot and heat through. It takes the noodles about 20 minute to cook. Serves 5.

CHICKEN FRICASSEE

1 can cream of chicken soup
½ soup can water
120 grams chopped onions
1 teaspoon paprika
1 teaspoon lemon juice

1 teaspoon rosemary
1 teaspoon thyme
1 teaspoon salt
1/4 teaspoon pepper
4 skinless boneless chicken breasts
non-stick cooking spray

Spray crockpot with non-stick cooking spray. Place chicken in crockpot. Mix remaining ingredients together and pour over chicken. Cover and cook on low setting for 6 to 8 hours. 1 hour before serving, prepare chive dumplings:

3 tablespoons. shortening
120 grams flour
2 teaspoons baking powder
¾ teaspoon salt
3 tablespoons fresh chopped chives, or 2 tablespoons dried chives
180 ml. skim milk

Mix dry ingredients and shortening. Add chives and milk, combine well. Drop by teaspoonfuls onto hot chicken and gravy. Cover and cook on high setting for 45-60 minutes. Serve with mashed potatoes and vegetables, or over hot, cooked noodles.

CHICKEN PARMIGIANA

3 chicken breasts
1 egg
1 teaspoon salt
¼ teaspoon pepper
20 grams dry bread crumbs
60 grams butter
1 can pizza sauce
6 slices mozzarella cheese
parmesan cheese

If using whole chicken breasts, cut into halves. In bowl beat egg, salt and pepper. Dip chicken into egg, then coat with crumbs. In large frying pan sauté chicken in butter. Arrange chicken in crockpot. Pour pizza sauce over chicken. Cover and cook on low setting for 6 to 8 hours. Add mozzarella cheese, sprinkle parmesan cheese on top. Cover and cook 15 minutes. Makes 6 servings.

CHICKEN MERLOT WITH MUSHROOMS

1.1 to 1.3 kilos meaty chicken pieces, skinned
340 grams sliced fresh mushrooms
1 large onion, chopped
2 cloves garlic, crushed
190 ml. chicken broth
1 x 170 gram can tomato paste
60 ml. dry red wine or chicken broth
2 tablespoons. quick-cooking tapioca
2 tablespoons snipped fresh basil or
1 ½ teaspoon dried basil, crushed
2 teaspoon sugar
¼ teaspoon salt
¼ teaspoon pepper
140 grams hot cooked noodles
2 tablespoons finely-grated
Parmesan cheese

Rinse chickenand set aside. In a large slow cooker place mushrooms, onion, and garlic. Place chicken pieces on top of the vegetables. In a bowl combine broth, tomato paste, wine or chicken broth, tapioca, dried basil (if using), sugar, salt, and pepper. Pour over everything. Coverand cook on low setting for 7 to 8 hours or on high setting for 3 ½ to 4 hours. If using, stir in fresh basil. To serve, spoon chicken, mushroom mixture, and sauce over hot cooked noodles Sprinkle with Parmesan cheese. Makes 4 to 6 servings.

CHICKEN OR TURKEY PIE

680 grams diced cooked chicken or turkey
2 cans (400 grams each) chicken broth
½ teaspoon salt
½ teaspoon pepper
1 stalk celery, thinly sliced
1 medium onion, chopped
1 bay leaf
675 grams potatoes, peeled and cubed

1 packet frozen mixed vegetables (450 grams)
250 ml. milk
120 grams flour
1 teaspoon pepper
½ teaspoon salt
1 x 9-inch refrigerated pie crust

In slow cooker, combine chicken, broth, ½ teaspoon salt, ½ teaspoon pepper, celery, onion, bay leaf, potatoes, and mixed vegetables. Cover and cook on low setting for 8 to 10 hours or on high setting for 4 to 6 hours. Remove bay leaf. Pre heat oven to 400° F. In a small bowl, mix milk and flour. Gradually stir flour and water mixture into crockpot. Stir in pepper, poultry seasoning, and salt. Remove the liner from crockpot base and carefully place 9-inch pie crust over the mixture. Place the crockery liner inside preheated oven and bake (uncovered) for about 15 minutes, or until browned. If your crockpot liner is not removable, put the mixture in a casserole dish, cover with the pie crust and bake as above. Serves 8.

CHICKEN PIZZA

4 skinless, boneless chicken breasts, cut into bite size pieces
1 onion, chopped
1 green bell pepper, chopped
2 large cans tomato sauce
2 large cans diced tomatoes
1 tablespoon dried parsley
1 tablespoon dried oregano
1 tablespoon dried basil
1 teaspoon thyme
4 cloves garlic, crushed
1 bay leaf

Place all ingredients in slow cooker. Stir to make sure all chicken is coated well. Cook on low setting for 8 hours, until chicken and vegetables are tender.

CHICKEN SOUP

2 onions, chopped
3 carrots, sliced
2 stalks celery, sliced
2 teaspoons salt
¼ teaspoon pepper
½ teaspoon basil
¼ teaspoon thyme
3 tablespoons dry parsley flakes
285 grams frozen peas
1 x 1.5 kg. whole chicken
1.2 litres water or chicken stock
225 grams noodles

Place all ingredients except noodles in slow cooker, in order listed. Cover and cook on low setting for 8 to 10 hours, or on high setting for 4 to 6 hours. One hour before serving, remove chicken and cool slightly. Remove meat from bones and return meat to slow cooker. Add noodles and turn to high setting. Cover and cook 1 hour.

CHICKEN STEW

900 grams chicken breasts/skinless Boneless/ cut into 1 inch cubes
500 ml. fat-free chicken broth
600 grams potatoes, peeled and cubed
450 grams finely-chopped onion
450 grams celery, sliced
225 grams carrots, sliced thin
1 teaspoon paprika
½ teaspoon pepper
½ teaspoon rubbed sage
½ teaspoon dried thyme
170 grams tomato paste
65 ml. cold water
3 tablespoons cornflour

In a slow cooker, combine the first 11 ingredients; cover and cook on high setting for 4 hours. Mix water and cornflour until smooth; stir into stew. Cook, covered, for a further 30 minutes or until the vegetables are tender. Serve 10.

CHICKEN STROGANOFF

250 ml. sour cream
1 tablespoon flour
35 grams chicken gravy mix
250 ml. water
450 grams. boneless, skinless chicken breast halves, cut into 1 inch pieces
1 x bag frozen "stew pack" vegetables, thawed
1 jar sliced mushrooms, drained
150 grams frozen peas, thawed
120 grams Bisquick
4 green onions, chopped
120 ml. milk

Mix sour cream, flour, gravy mix and water in 3 a large crockpot until smooth. Stir in chicken, stew vegetables and mushrooms. Cover and cook on low setting for 4 hours or until chicken is tender and sauce is thickened. Stir in peas. Mix baking mix and onions. Stir in milk just until moistened. Drop dough by rounded tablespoonfuls onto chicken-vegetable mixture. Cover and cook on high setting for 45 to 50 minutes or until toothpick inserted in centre of dumplings comes out clean. Serve immediately.

CHICKEN STEW MEXICAN STYLE

900 grams skinless boneless chicken breasts cut into 1½ pieces
4 medium russet potatoes, peeled and cut very small
1 x 425 gram can mild salsa
1 x 115 gram can diced green chillies
1 packet taco seasoning mix
1 x 230 gram can tomato sauce

Mix all ingredients together in crockpot, cook for 7 to 9 hours on low setting. Serve with warm flour tortillas.

CHICKEN THIGHS

6 chicken thighs (skinless)
1 can Italian-style diced tomatoes
salt and pepper

Throw these in the crockpot and cook on high setting for about 3 hours. Serve with egg noodles.

CHICKEN WINGS

2.25 kilos chicken wings
500 grams brown sugar
225 grams French mustard
4 tablespoons soy sauce

Cut each wing into 3 pieces, and throw away the tip. Brown in frying pan until golden brown and put in slow cooker. Turn on low heat. Mix brown sugar, mustard and soy sauce in saucepan and heat until it becomes liquid. Pour over the wings and cook for 8 hours on low setting.

CHICKEN TORTILLAS

meat from 1 whole chicken
1 can cream of chicken soup
115 grams green chilli salsa
2 tablespoons quick-cooking tapioca
1 medium onion, chopped
150 grams grated cheese
1 dozen corn tortillas
black olives

Tear chicken into bite size pieces, mix with soup, chilli, salsa and tapioca. Line bottom of crockpot with 3 corn tortillas, torn into bite size pieces. Add 1/3 of the chicken mixture. Sprinkle with 1/3 of the onion and 1/3 of the grated cheese. Repeat layers of tortillas topped with chicken mixture, onions and cheese. Cover and cook on low setting for 6 to 8 hours or on high setting for 3 hours. Garnish with sliced black olives.

CHILLI CHICKEN

3 whole chicken breasts cut in 1 inch pieces
150 grams chopped onion
150 grams chopped bell pepper
2 garlic cloves
2 tablespoons vegetable oil
2 cans stewed tomatoes
1 can chilli beans
170 grams piquant sauce
1 teaspoon chilli powder
1 teaspoon cumin
½ teaspoon salt

Sauté chicken, onion, pepper and garlic in vegetable oil until vegetables are wilted. Transfer to slow cooker and add remaining ingredients. Cook, covered, on low setting for 4 to 6 hours. Serve over rice. Serves 4 to 6.

CHICKEN WINGS IN BARBECUE SAUCE

1.5 kg. chicken wings
salt and pepper to taste
375 ml. any variety barbecue sauce
60 ml. honey
2 teaspoons prepared mustard or spicy mustard
2 teaspoons Worcestershire sauce
Tabasco to taste (optional)

Rinse chicken and pat dry. Cut off and discard wing tips. Cut each wing at joint to make two sections. Sprinkle wing parts with salt and pepper. Place wings on a broiler pan. Broil 4 to 5 inches from the heat for 20 minutes, 10 minutes for each side or until chicken is brown. Transfer chicken to slow cooker. For sauce, combine barbecue sauce, honey, mustard, Worcester-shire sauce and, if more heat is desired, Tabasco to taste, in a small mixing bowl. Pour over chicken wings. Cover and cook on low setting for 4 to 5 hours or on high for 2 to 2½ hours. Serve directly from slow cooker.

COQ AU VIN

12 small white onions, peeled
1.8 kilos roasting chicken, cut up
½ teaspoon salt
¼ teaspoon black pepper
65 ml. brandy or cognac
2 cloves garlic, peeled and crushed
¼ teaspoon ground thyme
1 bay leaf
375 ml. dry red wine
5 tablespoons flour
250 ml. chicken stock
2 kilos fresh mushrooms, wiped and stemmed
1 tablespoon butter or margarine
¼ teaspoon salt
1 tablespoon chopped fresh parsley

Place the onions in the slow cooker. Remove the fat from the vent of the chicken and dice it. In a large frying pan over medium heat, heat the fat until it is rendered. Discard the shriveled bits and sauté the chicken until well browned. Season with ½ teaspoon salt and pepper. Warm the brandy in a ladle or a small saucepan; light it with match and pour it over the chicken. When the flame dies, lift the chicken into the slow cooker and add the garlic, thyme, and bay leaf. Pour the wine into the hot frying pan and scrape up the pan juices. Dissolve the flour in the stock, turn it into the frying pan and bring to simmering, stirring briskly to prevent lumps. Turn into the slow cooker. Cover and cook on low setting for 7-9 hours. About 10 minutes before serving, in a medium frying pan, sauté the mushrooms in the butter over medium high heat. In about 5 minutes, they will be tender and the moisture will have evaporated from the frying pan. Season with ¼ teaspoon salt and add to the chicken casserole. If the sauce seems thin, simmer it in the frying pan long enough to thicken to the consistency of heavy cream. Garnish the Coq au Vin with parsley before serving.

CHICKEN WITH CHEESE SAUCE

Place two thawed chicken breast halves in crockpot. Mix together one can cream of chicken soup and half soup can of white wine; pour over chicken. Place two slices of Swiss cheese over top of chicken breasts (processed cheese melts and blends more easily). Cook in crockpot for 2 to 3 hours on high setting or for 3 to 4 hours on low setting. Serve over steamed rice. Serves 2.

CHICKEN WINGS IN TERIYAKI SAUCE

1.5 kg. chicken wings
1 large onion, chopped
250 ml. soy sauce
225 grams brown sugar
2 teaspoons ground ginger
2 cloves garlic, crushed
60 ml. dry cooking sherry

Rinse chicken and pat dry. Cut off and discard wing tips. Cut each wing at joint to make two sections. Place wing parts on broiler pan. Broil 4-5 inches from the heat for 20 minutes, 10 minutes for each side or until chicken is brown. Transfer chicken to slow cooker. Mix together onion, soy sauce, brown sugar, ginger, garlic and cooking sherry in bowl. Pour over chicken wings. Cover and cook on low setting for 5 to 6 hours or on high setting for 2 to 3 hours. Stir chicken wings once to ensure wings are evenly coated with sauce. Serve from slow cooker. Makes about 32 pieces

COUNTRY CAPTAIN CHICKEN BREASTS

2 medium-size Granny Smith apples
1 small onion, finely chopped
1 small green bell pepper, seeded and finely chopped
3 cloves garlic, crushed
2 tablespoons dried currants
1 tablespoon curry powder
1 teaspoon ground ginger
¼ teaspoon ground cayenne pepper
1 x 400 gram can diced tomatoes
6 small skinless, boneless chicken breast halves (about 800 grams total)
120 ml. chicken broth
225 grams long-grain white rice
450 grams large raw prawns, shelled and deveined
85 grams slivered almonds
salt
chopped parsley

Quarter, core, and dice unpeeled apples. In a large slow cooker combine apples, onion, bell pepper, garlic, currants, curry powder, ginger, and red pepper; stir in tomatoes. Rinse chicken and pat dry; then arrange, overlapping pieces slightly, on top of tomato mixture. Pour in broth. Cover and cook for 6 to 7 hours on low setting until chicken is very tender when pierced. Carefully lift chicken to a warm plate, cover lightly, and keep warm in a 200°F. oven. Stir rice into cooking liquid. Increase cooker to high heat setting; cover and cook, stirring once or twice, until rice is almost tender to bite (30 to 35 minutes). Stir in prawns, cover and cook until prawns are opaque in center; cut to test (about 10 more minutes). Meanwhile, toast almonds in a small nonstick frying pan over medium heat until golden brown (5 to 8 minutes), stirring occasionally. Set aside. To serve, season rice mixture to taste with salt. Mound in a warm serving dish; arrange chicken on top. Sprinkle with parsley and almonds. Makes 6 servings.

CREOLE CHICKEN

8 chicken thighs (or 3 large breasts)
1 can diced tomatoes
1 can tomato paste
1 chopped bell pepper
1 chopped onion
1 thick slice chopped ham
diced sausage
Tabasco sauce to taste

-Throw everything into the crockpot and cook on low setting for 4 to 5 hours. Towards the end of cooking time, thicken with a little cornflour, if desired. Delicious served over brown rice.

CRANBERRY CHICKEN

1 small onion, thinly sliced
225 grams fresh or frozen (unthawed) cranberries
12 skinless, boneless chicken thighs (about 1 kg. total)
60 ml. ketchup
2 tablespoons firmly packed brown sugar
1 teaspoon dry mustard
2 teaspoons cider vinegar
1½ tablespoons cornflour blended with 2 tablespoons cold water
salt

In a slow cooker, combine onion and cranberries. Arrange chicken on top. In small bowl, mix ketchup, sugar, mustard and vinegar and pour over chicken. Cover and cook on low setting for 6½ to 7½ hours, until chicken is very tender when pierced. Lift out chicken when cooked, and blend cornflour mixture into cooking liquid. Increase cooker heat setting to high; cover and cook for a further 10 to 15 minutes, stirring 2 or 3 times until sauce thickens. Season to taste with salt, and pour over chicken. Makes 6 servings.

COUNTRY CHICKEN STEW WITH BASIL DUMPLINGS

12 small white onions
water
450 grams boneless, skinless chicken thighs
450 grams boneless, skinless chicken breast halves
½ tablespoon chopped fresh basil leaves (or ½ teaspoon dried basil, crumbled)
salt and pepper to taste
1 large red bell pepper cut into 1 inch squares
4 cloves garlic, thinly sliced
500 ml. canned chicken broth
80 ml. dry white wine
2 tablespoons plain flour
2 tablespoons butter at room temperature
450 grams fresh asparagus, cut into 1½ inch lengths

DUMPLINGS:
240 ml. buttermilk and baking mix
80 ml. whole milk
60 grams chopped fresh basil leaves (or 1 tablespoon dried basil, crumbled)

Using a sharp knife, make a small "X" in the root end of each onion. Bring a saucepan of water to the boil. Add the onions, lower the heat, and simmer for 5 minutes. Drain and rinse under running cold water. Slip skins off onions. Rinse chicken and pat dry. Quarter the thighs and chicken breast halves. Stir in basil and seasonings with salt and pepper. Put chicken pieces in a large slow-cooker. Top with onions, bell peppers, and garlic. Pour in stock, and wine. DO NOT stir. Cover and cook on low setting for 6 to 8 hours or high setting for 2 to 2½ hours. Stir the stew. If cooking on low, change setting to high. In a small bowl, blend together the flour and butter. Stir into slow cooker and cook, stirring for about 5 minutes, until sauce begins to thicken. Stir in asparagus. In medium bowl, combine dumpling ingredients until evenly moistened. Drop by Tablespoons onto hot stew in 6 small rounds. Cover and cook for another 25 to 30 minutes, until dumplings are cooked through. Serve immediately!

CRANBERRY-APPLE TURKEY BREAST

2 teaspoons melted butter or margarine
120 ml. chicken broth
1 large apple, cored and chopped
120 grams chopped onion
1 stalk celery, chopped
250 ml. whole berry cranberry sauce
¾ teaspoon poultry seasoning
400 grams seasoned crumb-style stuffing
1.5 kg. turkey breast cutlets

Combine butter, chicken broth, apple, onion, celery, cranberry sauce, poultry seasoning and stuffing. Place 3 tablespoons stuffing mix on each turkey cutlet. Roll up and tie. Place in slow cooker. Cover and cook on low setting for 8 hours, or on high setting for 4 hours.

CREAM CHEESE CHICKEN

1 frying chicken, cut up
2 tablespoons melted butter
salt and pepper to taste
1 pkt. dry Italian seasoning mix
1 can cream of chicken soup
225 grams cream cheese, cut into cubes
125 ml. chicken broth
1 large onion
crushed garlic to taste

Brush chicken with butter and sprinkle with the dry Italian seasoning mix. Cover and cook on low setting for 6 to 7 hours. About 45 minutes before done, brown the onion in the butter and then add the cream cheese, soup, and chicken broth to the saucepan. Add the crushed garlic and stir all ingredients until smooth. Add salt and pepper to taste. Pour sauce mixture over chicken in the crockpot and cook for an additional 30-45 minutes. Remove chicken to platter and stir sauce before putting in gravy.

CROCKPOT CHICKEN

1 frying chicken, cut up
salt and pepper
1 can cream of mushroom soup
115 grams Sauterne or sherry
2 tablespoons butter or margarine, melted
2 tablespoons dry Italian salad dressing mix
2 x 85 grams packets cream cheese, cut in cubes
1 tablespoon chopped onion

Wash chicken and pat dry. Brush with butter. Sprinkle with salt and pepper. Place in crockpot. Sprinkle with dry salad mix. Cover and cook on low for 5 to 6 hours. About ¾ hour before serving, mix soup, cream cheese, wine, and onion in small saucepan. Cook until smooth. Pour over chicken in pot. Cover and cook for 30 minutes on low. Serve with sauce. Serve with rice or noodles. Serves 4 to 6.

CREAMY CHICKEN DINNER

4 boneless / skinless chicken breasts
seasoned with garlic powder,
onion powder and seasoned salt
1 large can cream of chicken soup
2 cans cream of mushroom soup
200 grams frozen cut carrots
200 grams frozen green beans

Place all of the ingredients in the crockpot and cook for about 7 hours on low. Add 160 grams of minute rice in the last 5 minutes before serving.

FIESTA CHICKEN

2 tablespoons oil
1.5 kg. boneless, skinless chicken breasts, cut into 1-inch pieces
1 medium onion, chopped

1 teaspoon oregano
1 small jalapeno pepper, finely chopped
3 cloves garlic, crushed
1 large can Mexican style diced tomatoes
¼ teaspoon ground cumin

Heat oil in frying pan. Cook chicken pieces until browned. Remove and drain. Place onion, green bell pepper, garlic and jalapeno pepper in frying pan and sauté until slightly cooked. Add all ingredients to crockpot and stir to combine. Cover and cook on low setting for 8 hours or on high setting for 4 hours. Serve on flour tortillas.

GARLIC CHICKEN WITH CABBAGE

1 whole chicken
1whole red or white onion, chopped
3 to 8 garlic cloves (or use garlic salt or powder to taste)
salt and pepper to taste

Season chicken and place in slow cooker. Add onion and garlic cloves and salt and pepper. Fill slow cooker a quarter of the way with water, cover and cook on high setting for 6 to 8 hours. The chicken should fall off of the bone. During the last hour of cooking the chicken, cut up 1 head of green cabbage. Place in a large saucepan with a shallow amount of water. Add two tablespoons of butter or margarine and sprinkle liberally with garlic salt and pepper. Cover and cook on medium-high heat for 20-30 minutes. Once chicken and cabbage are done, place some cabbage in a bowl and top with chicken and some of the chicken broth. You can alter any of the seasonings and the butter or margarine to your liking.

GARLIC ROASTED CHICKEN

2.25 kg. roasting chicken
salt
pepper
paprika
5 garlic cloves, minced
¼ pound sweet butter
125 ml. chicken broth

Sprinkle the chicken, inside and out, with salt, pepper and paprika. Spread half of the garlic in the cavity and spread the rest on the outside of the bird. Place the bird in the slow cooker and place a few pats of butter on its breast. Add the remaining ingredients and cook on low setting for 6 to 8 hours. Serve the garlic butter sauce with the chicken.

GREEK CHICKEN

6 skinless chicken breasts
1 large can tomato sauce
1 small can tomato purée
1 can sliced mushrooms
1 can ripe olives
1 tablespoon garlic
1 tablespoon lemon juice
1 teaspoon oregano
1 onion, chopped
125 ml. wine or brandy (optional)
500 grams rice
salt to taste

Wash and remove fat from chicken. Bake in 350°F degree oven for about an hour. Meanwhile, combine all other ingredients except rice). Put chicken and sauce in a slow cooker on low heat and cook for at least 4 hours to blend flavours. Before serving, cook rice according to directions on box. Serve chicken and sauce over rice. Serves 6.

GREEN CHILLI-STUFFED CHICKEN BREASTS

4 boneless, skinned chicken breast halves, pounded thin
3 ounces cream cheese
170 grams grated cheddar cheese
115 grams green chillis
½ teaspoon chilli powder
salt and pepper to taste
1 can cream of mushroom soup
120 ml. hot enchilada sauce

Combine cream cheese, grated cheese, chillies, chilli powder and salt and pepper. Place a generous dollop on each flattened chicken breast, then roll up. Place chicken rolls in the crockpot, seam-side down. Top chicken breast rolls with remaining cheese mixture, soup, and enchilada sauce. Cover and cook on low setting for 6 to 7 hours. Serves 4. With the cheese mixture in the centre, these chicken breasts come out tender and moist.

HEALTHY CROCKPOT CHICKEN CREOLE

1.4 kg. chicken thighs or breasts, skinned
150 grams celery, diced
1 red bell pepper, sliced
1 green bell pepper, sliced
1 onion, sliced
1 can sliced mushrooms
1 can tomatoes
1 teaspoon garlic powder
3 sachets sugar substitute
1 teaspoon Cajun seasoning
½ teaspoon paprika
salt and pepper to taste
hot sauce to taste
160 grams minute rice, cooked

Place chicken in bottom of your slow cooker. Combine remaining ingredients (except rice) and add to slow cooker. Cook on high setting for 4 to 5 hours or on low setting for 7 to 8 hours. Cook rice according to packet direction. Spoon Creole mixture over hot cooked rice.

HONEYED CHICKEN WINGS

1.4 kg. chicken wings
salt and pepper, to taste
250 ml. honey
125 ml. soy sauce
2 tablespoon vegetable oil
2 tablespoon ketchup
1/2 garlic cloves, crushed

Cut off and discard chicken wing tips. Cut each wing into 2 parts and sprinkle with salt and pepper. Combine remaining ingredients and mix well. Place wings in slow cooker and pour sauce over. Cook on low setting for 6 to 8 hours.

LAZY CROCKPOT CHICKEN

1 packet boneless chicken breasts
1 can cream of mushroom soup
60 grams. flour
1 jar sliced mushrooms
salt, pepper and paprika

Rinse chicken breasts. Put salt, pepper and paprika on both sides. Place in crockpot. Mix other ingredients together, and add to crockpot. Cook on setting all day. Serve over noodles, rice, or mashed potatoes.

HOT CHICKEN SANDWICHES

12 eggs
1 loaf of bread (cubed)
2 large (or 3 small) chickens (reserve some broth for use in recipe)
salt to taste
pepper to taste

Boil the chickens until cookded and allow to cool. When the chicken meat is completely cool to the touch, pick the chicken meat from the bones and set aside. Reserve a little of the broth for later. Cube the loaf of bread and put it in a large bowl. Mix in the 12 eggs with the cubed bread. Add the chicken meat you picked from the bone and enough broth from the chicken to moisten. Add salt and pepper to your own taste. Mix well. Spread mixture into a lightly greased casserole dish and bake in a preheated 350°F (175°C) oven for 30 minutes. Or spray a slow cooker with cooking spray to prevent sticking and pour in the chicken mixture. Cook on low setting for about 6 hours. Serve by scooping onto buns. Makes 12 to 18 servings

JAMBALAYA

450 grams boneless chicken breasts, cut into one inch cubes
450 grams smoked sausage, sliced
450 grams prawns, cooked
2 cans crushed tomatoes
1 medium onion, chopped
1 green pepper, chopped
250 ml. chicken broth
120 ml. white wine
2 teaspoons oregano
2 teaspoons parsley
2 teaspoons Cajun seasoning
1 teaspoon cayenne pepper
160 grams rice, cooked

Cut chicken and slice sausage. Chop onion and green pepper. Put all in slow cooker. Add remaining ingredients, except prawns and rice. Cook in crockpot on low setting for 6 to 8 hours. 30 minutes before eating, add cooked prawns and cooked rice; allow to heat. Can be cooked on high setting for 3 to 4 hours instead.

JERK CHICKEN

1 large onion, cut into 8 pieces
1 generous tablespoon chopped crystallised ginger
½ to 1 habanera pepper, seeded, de-veined, and finely crushed (wear gloves!)
½ teaspoon ground mixed spice
2 tablespoons dry mustard
1 teaspoon freshly ground black pepper
2 tablespoons red wine or balsamic vinegar
2 tablespoons soy sauce
2 cloves garlic, crushed and minced
1.8 kg. chicken breasts

This is a traditional Jamaican dish adapted for the crockpot. Combine onion and ginger in a food processor; process until finely chopped. Add remaining ingredients, except chicken, and pulse until well combined. Place chicken in a large slow cooker and cover with sauce. Cover, set on low, and cook for 6 to 8 hours. or until chicken is tender (3 to 4 hours on high setting). 4 servings.

LEMON BAKED CHICKEN

450 grams skinned and boned uncooked chicken breasts, cut into 4 pieces
1 lemon
1 teaspoon lemon pepper
1 teaspoon paprika

Place chicken pieces in a slow cooker. Squeeze juice of half a lemon over chicken. Sprinkle lemon pepper and paprika over top. Cut remaining lemon half into thin slices. Arrange slices around chicken. Cover and cook on high setting for 4 hours.

LEMON-GARLIC CHICKEN

1.5 kg. chicken
120 ml. lemon juice
120 grams garlic cloves, crushed
1 teaspoon seasoned salt
1 teaspoon poultry seasoning
2 dashes Tabasco
250 ml. white wine

Skin and cut up chicken. Combine with other ingredients in slow cooker. Cook on low setting all day (about 8 hours). Upon return from work, de-bone the chicken, and serve over rice.

LEMON-ROSEMARY CHICKEN

125 ml. lemon juice
1 tablespoon vegetable oil
1 garlic clove, crushed
1 teaspoon. dried rosemary
¼ teaspoon. salt
¼ easpoon. pepper
900 grams boneless, skinless chicken breasts

In a large food storage bag, place lemon juice, oil, garlic, rosemary, salt and pepper. Add chicken. Close bag and marinate in refrigerator 4 hours or overnight, turning bag frequently. Place chicken in the slow cooker and pour marinade over. Cover and cook for 6 to 8 hours on low setting, or until tender, basting occasionally with the marinade, if possible. You may add frozen broccoli and carrots about 1 to 1½ hours before the chicken is cooked. Serves 4 to 6.

LEMON TARRAGON CHICKEN WITH ASPARAGUS

450 grams frozen chicken breasts, boneless
60 ml. lemon juice
60 ml. chicken stock
1 teaspoon tarragon (dried)
1 packet frozen asparagus (or fresh partially cooked)
2 tablespoons flour
120 ml. double cream
salt and pepper to taste

Put frozen chicken breasts in crockpot and add lemon juice, broth, and tarragon. Cook on low 6 hours. Add asparagus; whisk cream and flour together and add. Cook another hour on high or until asparagus is tender and sauce is thickened. Serve over noodles or rice. Artichokes are good in this too!

LO-CAL CROCKPOT CHICKEN

2 medium onions, thinly sliced
1.4 kilos chicken, cut up and skinned
2 cloves garlic, crushed
1 large can tomatoes
1 teaspoon salt
¼ teaspoon pepper
½ teaspoon oregano, crushed
½ teaspoon basil
½ teaspoon celery seed
1 bay leaf

Layer in order and cook on low 6-8 hours, or on high 2 1/2 - 4 hours.

LOW-FAT CHICKEN & VEGGIE BAKE

8 boneless, skinless chicken breasts
2 cans whole potatoes, drained
1 teaspoon garlic powder
1 bottle fat-free Italian salad dressing
1 packet frozen vegetables
1 can water chestnuts (optional)
salt and pepper

Sprinkle chicken breasts with salt, pepper and garlic. Put chicken in bottom of slow cooker. Add remaining ingredients. Cook on high setting for 4 to 6 hours or on low for 8 ti 10 hours. Serves 8

LOW-FAT GLAZED CHICKEN IN SLOW COOKER

170 grams orange juice concentrate
3 chicken breasts, split
½ teaspoon marjoram
1 dash ground nutmeg
1 dash garlic powder (optional)
60 ml. water
2 tablespoon cornflour

Combine thawed orange juice concentrate (not ordinary orange juice) in bowl along with the marjoram, garlic powder and nutmeg. Split the chicken breasts to make 6 serving sizes. Dip pieces into the orange juice to coat completely. Place in crockpot. Pour the remaining orange juice mixture over the chicken. Cover and cook on low setting for 7 to 9 hours, or on high for 4 hours if you wish. When chicken is cooked remove to serving platter. Pour the sauce that remains into a saucepan. Mix the cornflour and water and stir into the juice in the saucepan. Cook over medium heat, stirring constantly, until thick and bubbly. Serve the sauce over the chicken.

LEMON PEPPER CHICKEN

5 boneless skinless chicken breasts (or any chicken pieces)
lemon pepper seasoning
2 tablespoon. melted margarine

Put chicken in slow cooker. Sprinkle generously with seasoning. Pour margarine over chicken. Cook on setting for 10 hours on high for 6 hours.

MAPLE-FLAVOURED BARBECUE CHICKEN

250 ml. ketchup
125 ml. maple-flavoured syrup
2 tablespoons prepared mustard
2 tablespoons Worcestershire sauce
2 teaspoon lemon juice
½ teaspoon chilli powder
¼ teaspoon garlic powder
4 boneless, skinned chicken breasts

Place all ingredients in slow cooker and cook on low setting for about 7 to 8 hours or until chicken is done. Remove meat, shred and return to sauce. Place on buns for sandwiches or serve over hot rice. Serves 4 to 6.

MEDITERRANEAN STYLE CHICKEN

6 skinless and boneless chicken breasts
1 large can tomato sauce
1 small can tomato purée
1 can sliced mushrooms
1 can ripe olives, sliced or whole
1 tablespoon garlic
1 tablespoon lemon juice
1 teaspoon oregano
1 onion, chopped
120 ml. wine or brandy (optional)

cooked rice
salt to taste

Wash and remove excess fat from chicken. Combine all ingredients in the slow cooker except the rice. Cover and cook on low setting for 6 to 8 hours. Serve chicken and sauce over rice. Serves 6.

MEXICAN CHICKEN

chicken pieces
taco seasoning

Cook all day on low setting or several hours on high. Serve as chicken tacos or with a side dish or as the main course. Super simple. You really cannot go wrong. Be careful because if you cook too long the bones could come apart into small pieces and could be difficult to separate from meat.

ONE POT CHICKEN AND GRAVY

boneless, skinless chicken breasts
potatoes, quartered, with jackets
about 6 stalks celery
½ packet baby carrots
1 can cream of chicken soup
1 packet dry onion soup mix

Place vegetables on bottom of crockpot. Brown chicken breasts in oil or vegetable spray. Place over vegetables. Cover with the cream of chicken soup, undiluted. Sprinkle with dry onion soup mix. Do not add water. Cover and cook all day on low setting , or for 6 hours on high.

PHILIPPINE CHICKEN

1 chicken, cut up
250 ml. water
120 ml. vinegar
60 ml. soy sauce
2 cloves garlic, sliced

Put all ingredients in crockpot and cook for 6 to 8 hours on low setting. Serve over rice.

PHEASANT AND WILD RICE

225 grams raw wild rice
1 can cream of mushroom soup
1 can cream of chicken soup
1 can mushrooms
240 ml. water
2 pheasants, cut up, floured and browned
1 packet instant onion soup mix

Mix rice, canned soup, water, mushrooms and water together in slow cooker. Place pheasants in slow cooker and sprinkle with onion soup mix. Cover. Cook on low setting for 6 to 8 hours. Add a splash more water if rice is looking dry towards end of cooking time.

ORANGE BURGUNDY CHICKEN

1.5 kg. frying chicken, cut up
120 ml. orange marmalade
120 ml. orange juice
120 ml. dry red wine
2 tablespoons cornflour
2 tablespoons brown sugar, packed
1 tablespoon lemon juice
1 teaspoon salt

Remove skin from chicken. Rinse and place in slow cooker. Combine remaining ingredients in a bowl and pour over chicken. Cover and cook on low setting for 6 to 8 hours. Serve with rice and spinach salad. Serves 6.

SPAGHETTI SAUCE WITH CHICKEN & SAUSAGE

450 grams. Italian sausage
3-4 boneless chicken breasts, cut into 1-inch chunks
150 grams chopped green pepper
150 grams chopped onion
1 to 2 teaspoons Italian seasoning
2 x 115 gram cans mushroom stems and pieces, drained
2 jars of your favourite spaghetti sauce
hot, cooked pasta

In a frying pan brown Italian sausage, piercing skins to allow excess fat to run out. Remove to plate and cut into ½ to 1-inch chunks. In the same frying pan, brown chicken pieces. Place sausage and chicken in slow cooker. Add pepper and onion. Sprinkle with Italian seasoning. Add mushrooms. Pour sauce over everything. Cover and cook on low setting for 6 to 8 hours. Stir before serving over spaghetti or other pasta.

ORANGE-GLAZED CHICKEN

170 grams orange juice concentrate
6 chicken breast halves
½ teaspoon marjoram
1 dash ground nutmeg
1 dash garlic powder
60 ml. water
2 tablespoons cornflour

Combine orange juice concentrate in a bowl with the marjoram, garlic powder and nutmeg. Dip each chicken breast half into the orange juice to coat completely, and place in slow cooker. Pour the remaining orange juice mixture over the chicken. Cover and cook on low setting for 6-8 hours, or on high for about 4 hours.

PROVINCIAL CHICKEN

650 grams chicken breasts
2 small zucchinis, diced
1 x 115 gram can sliced black olives
1 tablespoon sherry wine vinegar or
balsamic vinegar
1 x 425 gram can diced tomatoes
1 can (285 grams) cream of chicken soup
with herbs
2 teaspoons dried parsley flakes
1 teaspoon dried basil
1 tablespoon dried minced onion
125 grams grated cheddar cheese
2 to 3 tablespoons sour cream (optional)
hot noodles, rice or pasta

Combine first 9 ingredients in a large slow cooker. Cover and cook on low setting for 6 to 8 hours. Add cheese and sour cream during the last 15 minutes. Serve over hot noodles, rice or pasta.

SPANISH CHICKEN

910 grams boneless skinless chicken
breasts (seasoned with salt and pepper
to taste)
black olives, pitted
sliced mushrooms, drained
stewed tomatoes
liquid to cover (beer, tomato soup or
tomato sauce with equal amount of
water or stock)

Cut chicken into bite-sized pieces; season. Place with remaining ingredients in slow cooker. Cook all day on low setting. Serve over rice. Serves 4.

SWEET AND SOUR CHICKEN

6 medium carrots, cut into ½ inch chunks

115 grams finely chopped green pepper
1 small onion, finely chopped
3 split chicken breasts (remove skin,
optional)
½ teaspoon salt
1 x 285 gram jar sweet and sour sauce
1 x 425 grams can pineapple chunks,
drained
2 tablespoons cornflour

Place all ingredients in slow cooker with chicken on top. Cover and cook on low setting for 6 to 8 hours. Remove chicken and thicken with 2 tablespoons cornflour dissolved to a medium thick paste with water. Pour over chicken breasts, or remove chicken from bone and cover with sauce mixture. Serve with steamed white or brown rice.

TURKEY BARBECUE

2 to 1.4 kilos turkey fillets
2 green peppers
1 teaspoon celery salt
Dash of pepper
2 teaspoon. chopped onion
1 bottle thick barbecue sauce

Prepare turkey fillets with dash of pepper across tops. Bake in 180°F oven for 1 hour covered. Uncover for desired darker colour. Prepare chopped green peppers, onions. Mix barbecue sauce, celery salt, (thin with water if needed) in a large crockpot, on high setting. Add green peppers and onions. Allow to heat while turkey is baking. Chop turkey into small to medium chunks and add to slow cooker. Cook for 4 to 6 hours on low setting. Serve on fresh rolls. Serves 4 to 6.

SWISS CHICKEN CASSEROLE

6 chicken breasts, boneless and skinless
6 slices Swiss cheese
1 can cream of mushroom soup
60 ml. milk
160 grams stuffing mix
20 grams butter or margarine, melted

Lightly grease crockpot or spray with cooking spray. Place chicken breasts in pot. Top with cheese. Combine soup and milk, stirring well. Spoon over cheese; sprinkle with stuffing mix. Drizzle melted butter over stuffing mix. Cook on low 8 to 10 hours or high 4 to 6 hours. Serves 6.

TERIYAKI SAUCE WINGS

1.5 kg. chicken wings
1 onion, chopped
250 ml. soy sauce
225 grams brown sugar
2 teaspoons ground ginger
2 cloves garlic, crushed
60 ml. dry sherry

Rinse chicken and pat dry. Cut off wing tips and discard. Cut each wing into 2 pieces, cutting at the joint. Broil wings 4 inches from heat for about 10 minutes on each side, or until browned. Transfer to Crockpot. Mix all remaining ingredients together and pour over chicken wings. Cook, covered, on low setting for 5 to 6 hours or on high setting for 2 to 3 hours. Stir once or twice to keep wings coated with sauce. Makes about 32 wings.

TURKEY A LA KING

300 grams cooked turkey or cooked chicken, cubed
100 grams sliced fresh mushrooms or canned mushrooms
2 cans cream of chicken soup

375 ml. cups milk
225 grams frozen peas
375 ml. sour cream

In crock pot mix together all ingredients except sour cream. Cook on low setting all day on low. About ½ hour before you serve add sour cream and mix well. When it comes back up to the desired temperature it is ready to serve. Serve over mashed potatoes, or slices of toast.

TURKEY AND RICE CASSEROLE

2 cans cream of mushroom soup
700 ml. water
600 grams converted long-grain white rice (uncooked)
150 grams thinly sliced celery
160 grams cubed cooked turkey
160 grams frozen mixed vegetables (peas & carrots, oriental mix, etc.)
1 teaspoon poultry seasoning
1 tablespoon dried minced onion

Pour soup and water into crockpot and stir to combine. Add remaining ingredients and mix well. Cover and cook for 6 to 8 hours on low setting or 3 to 4 hours on high. Add soy sauce if desired.

TURKEY MADEIRA

675 grams turkey breasts
60 grams porcini mushrooms (dried)
180 ml. chicken broth
3 tablespoons Madeira wine
1 tablespoon lemon juice
salt and pepper to taste

Cover and cook on low setting for 6 to 8 hours. Thicken juices with cornflour if desired, and serve with rice. Serves 4.

TURKEY MEATBALLS

350 ml. barbecue sauce
285 grams apple jam
2 tablespoons tapioca (for thick sauce if desired)
1 tablespoon vinegar
1 egg, beaten
60 grams seasoned fine bread crumbs
2 tablespoons milk
1/4 teaspoon Garlic powder
1/4 teaspoon salt
¼ teaspoon onion powder
450 grams minced turkey
non-stick vegetable spray

In a crockpot stir together barbecue sauce, jam, tapioca (if used), and vinegar. Cover and cook on high setting while preparing meatballs. For meatballs, in large bowl combine egg, bread crumbs, milk, garlic powder, salt, and onion powder. Add minced turkey and mix well. Shape into ½ to ¾ -inch meatballs. Spray a 12-inch non-stick frying pan; add meatballs and brown on all sides over medium heat. Drain meatballs and add them to the crockpot. Stir gently, cover and cook on high heat setting for 1½ to 2 hours. Makes 30 meatballs.

WINNING WINGS IN SWEET AND SOUR SAUCE

16 chicken wings
4 tablespoons wine or balsamic vinegar
150 grams apricot preserves
2 tablespoons peanut butter (optional)
250 ml. ketchup
4 tablespoons horseradish
150 grams sweet onion, finely chopped

1 teaspoon hot sauce (optional)

Pat the chicken wings dry and place then in the slow cooker. In a bowl, mix together remaining ingredients. Taste - check for a good balance of sweet and sour. Pour the sauce over the wings. Cover the slow cooker and cook on low setting for about 4 hours, until the chicken is tender

TURKEY SANDWICHES

1 kg. diced turkey
600 grams. diced cheese
1 can cream of mushroom soup
1 can cream of chicken soup
1 onion, chopped
125 ml. instant whip

Mix all of above and cook in a crockpot on high setting for 3 to 4 hours. Stir occasionally. Add liquid, if needed. Serve with buns.

YUMMY CHICKEN WINGS

12-18 chicken wings
85 ml. soy sauce
1 teaspoon ginger
2 garlic cloves minced
2 green onions minced
1 tablespoon honey
2 teaspoon oil

Combine ingredients in your crockpot. Cook on low setting for 6 to 8 hours serves 2-4 people depending on appetizer or main dish

VEGETARIAN

ALL DAY MACARONI CHEESE

230 grams elbow macaroni, cooked and drained
450 grams grated cheddar cheese
1 can evaporated milk
350 ml. milk
2 eggs
1 teaspoon salt
½ teaspoon black pepper

Place the cooked macaroni in a crockpot that has been sprayed with non-stick cooking spray. Add the remaining ingredients, except 150 grams of the cheese, and mix well. Sprinkle with the remaining cheese and then cover and cook on low setting for 5 to 6 hours or until the mixture is firm and golden around the edges. Do not remove the cover or stir until it has finished cooking.

ARTICHOKE & CHEESE DIP

450 grams. grated Mozzarella
225 grams grated Parmesan
240 ml. mayonnaise
230 gram jar artichoke hearts, drained and chopped

Mix ingredients together. Bake in casserole at 180°F for 20 to 30 minutes or in a lightly buttered slow cooker on high setting for about 1 hour. Serve with broken up French bread or wheat crackers.

ASPARAGUS CASSEROLE

2 x 280 ml. cans sliced asparagus
1 x 280 ml. can cream of celery soup
2 hard boiled eggs, thinly sliced
125 grams grated cheddar cheese
75 grams coarsely crushed Ritz crackers
1 teaspoon butter

Place drained asparagus in lightly buttered slow cooker. Combine soup and cheese. Top asparagus with sliced eggs, soup mixture, then the cracker crumbs. Dot with butter. Cover and cook on low setting for 4 to 6 hours.

BOSTON BAKED BEANS

450 grams small dry white beans
1 medium onion, chopped
4 slices bacon, chopped
65 ml. light (mild) molasses
60 grams packed dark brown sugar
2 teaspoons dry mustard
¼ teaspoon ground black pepper
1/8 teaspoon ground cloves
1½ teaspoons salt

Rinse beans with cold running water and discard any stones or shriveled beans. In a large bowl, place beans and enough water to cover by 2 inches. Cover and let stand at room temperature overnight. Drain and rinse beans. In a large crockpot stir 2 litres of water with the beans and remaining ingredients except salt until blended. Cover crockpot with lid and cook beans on low setting for about 14 hours or until beans are tender and sauce is syrupy. Stir salt into bean mixture before serving.

BAKED POTATOES

10 to 12 potatoes
aluminium foil

Prick potatoes with fork and wrap each in foil. Fill slow crockpot with potatoes. Cover and cook on low setting for 8 to 10 hours, or on high setting for 2 ¼to 4 hours. Do not add water.

BARLEY WITH MUSHROOMS AND GREEN ONIONS

150 grams barley
1 x 500 ml. can roasted garlic chicken broth
3 green onions, thinly sliced
4 to 6 ounces fresh or canned mushrooms, sliced
salt or seasoned salt and pepper to taste
2 teaspoons butter or margarine

Combine all ingredients in slow cooker/Crockpot. Cover and cook on low setting for 4 to 4½ hours.

BAVARIAN RED CABBAGE

1 large head of red cabbage, washed and coarsely sliced
2 medium onions coarsely chopped
6 tart apples, cored and quartered
2 teaspoons salt
500 ml. hot water
3 tablespoons sugar
160 ml. cider vinegar
6 tablespoons bacon fat or butter

Place all ingredients in the crockpot in the order listed. Cover and cook on low setting for 8 to 10 hours or on high setting for 3 hurs. Stir well before serving.

BREAKFAST CASSEROLE

4 medium-sized apples, peeled and sliced
60 ml. honey
1 teaspoon cinnamon
2 tablespoon. butter, melted
160 grams toasted muesli cereal

Place apples in slow cooker and mix in remaining ingredients. Cover and cook overnight on on low setting for 7 to 9 hours. Serve with milk.

CAPONATA

450 grams plum tomatoes chopped
1 eggplant (aubergine), cut into ½ inch pieces
2 medium zucchinis, cut into ½ inch pieces
1 onion, finely chopped
3 stalks celery, sliced
115 grams chopped parsley
2 tablespoons red wine vinegar
1 tablespoon brown sugar
60 grams raisins
65 ml. tomato paste
1 teaspoon salt
¼ teaspoon freshly ground black pepper
3 tablespoon oil cured black olives (optional)
2 tablespoon capers (optional)

Combine tomatoes, eggplant, zucchini, celery, onion, parsley, vinegar, sugar, raisins, tomato paste, salt and pepper in a crockpot. Cook, covered on low heat for 5½ hours. Do not remove cover during cooking. Stir in olives & capers, if using. Serve warm or cold.

BROCCOLI AND CHEESE SOUP

160 grams cooked noodles
340 grams broccoli
3 tablespoons. chopped onions
2 tablespoons. butter
1 tablespoons. flour
200 grams cheese
salt to taste
1400 ml. milk

Combine all ingredients in slow cooker. Stir well, and cook on low setting for 4 hours. Makes 8 servings.

BROCOLLI CASSEROLE

285 grams frozen chopped broccoli
6 eggs, beaten
680 grams cottage cheese
6 tablespoons flour
225 grams mild cheese of your choice, diced
¼ cup butter, melted
2 green onions, chopped
salt, to taste

Thaw broccoli in colander by running cold water over it for several minutes.Separate into pieces. Drain well. In a large bowl, combine remaining ingredients and mix well. Stir in broccoli. Pour into greased slow cooker. Cover. Cook on high for 1 hour. Stir well. Finish cooking on low setting for 2 to 4 hours.

BROCCOLI CHEESE WITH ALMONDS

680 grams fresh broccoli, trimmed well
1 x 285 gram can cream of chicken soup
½ cup mayonnaise
225 grams cheddar cheese (grated)
¼ cup toasted slivered almonds

Place broccoli in slow cooker sprayed with vegetable cooking spray. Combine chicken soup, mayonnaise, half of the cheese, and 1/4 cup water, and spoon over broccoli. Cover and cook on low for 2-3 hours. When ready to serve, sprinkle remaining cheese over broccoli, and top with slivered almonds.

BROCCOLI SOUFFLÉ

2 packets frozen chopped broccoli (907 grams)
1 can cream of celery soup (undiluted)
240 ml. mayonnaise
3 tablespoons grated onion
2 eggs, beaten
100 grams grated cheddar cheese
Ritz crackers
113 grams melted margarine

Cook broccoli; drain and cool. Mix soup, mayonnaise, onion, egg, and cheese and add to cooled broccoli. Put in a large, lightly-greased crockpot. Mix 1 stack Ritz or buttery crackers (crushed) with margarine or butter. Put on top. Cook on high setting for 2 to 3 hours.

BROCCOLI SOUP FOR THE CROCKPOT

1 litre water + 4 chicken stock cubes (or 1 litre of chicken stock)
50 grams onions, chopped
350 grams potatoes, diced
450 grams broccoli florets, chopped
800 ml cream of chicken soup
300 grams Cheddar cheese, grated

Add the water, stock cubes, onions, potatoes and broccoli to a slow cooker. Cook on high setting until the broccoli stars to soften (about 5 minutes). Add the cream of chicken soup and the cheese then turn the crockpot to low and continue cooking for about 2 hours.

CABBAGE CHILLI SOUP

600 grams coarsely chopped cabbage
150 grams chopped onions
600 grams tomato juice 1 (300 gram)
can tomato soup
1 x 300 gram can kidney beans,
rinsed and drained
2 teaspoons chilli seasoning mix

In a slow cooker, combine cabbage, onion, tomato juice and tomato soup. Add kidney beans and chilli seasoning mix. Mix well to combine. Cover and cook on low setting for 6 to 8 hours. Mix well before serving.

CARROTS WITH ORANGE GLAZE

3 cups sliced carrots
3 tablespoons butter
2 cups water
3 tablespoons orange marmalade
¼ teaspoon salt
2 tablespoons chopped pecans

Combine carrots, water, and salt in crockpot. Cover and cook on high setting for 2 to 3 hours or until the carrots are done. Drain well; stir in remaining ingredients. Cover and cook on high setting for a further 20 to 30 minutes. Makes 5 to 6 servings.

CHEDDAR POTATO SLICES

1 large can cream of mushroom soup
½ teaspoon paprika
½ teaspoon pepper
4 medium baking potatoes (about 1¼ pounds), sliced ¼ -inch thick
125 grams grated cheddar cheese

Mix all ingredients in a lightly greased slow cooker. Cover and cook on high setting for 3 to 4 hours, until potatoes are tender. Keep warm (on low) for serving.

CHEESE AND POTATO CASSEROLE

910 grams hash brown potatoes
2 cans cheddar cheese soup
1 can evaporated milk
1 can French fried onion rings, divided
salt and pepper to taste

Combine potatoes, soup, milk, and half the can of onion rings; pour into a greased slow cooker and add salt and pepper. Cover and cook on low setting for 8 to 9 hours or high setting for 4 hours. Sprinkle the rest of the onion rings of top before serving.

CHEESE & ARTICHOKE DIP

225 grams processed cheese
1 can cream of mushroom soup
2 teaspoons Worcestershire sauce
60 ml. evaporated milk
1 teaspoon dry mustard
150 grams grated cheddar cheese
85 grams chopped roasted red pepper
1 can artichoke hearts, drained and coarsely chopped

Combine all ingredients in the slow cooker. Cover and cook on low setting for 2 to 3 hours, until melted. Stir well and serve with assorted crackers, bread cubes, or chips. You can also use this dip with cooked pasta for a delicious macaroni cheese!

CHEESE DIP

910 grams cheese
2 cans tomatoes and chillies
1 can cream of mushroom soup
1 small jar piquant sauce
1 teaspoon garlic powder
dash of Worcestershire sauce
450 grams premium minced beef
1 medium onion, chopped
450 grams sausage

Mix all of the liquids and cheese together in a crockpot set on low until the cheese melts. While this is cooking, brown meats and chopped onion. Drain fat off of meats and add spices, then add to crockpot and stir. Cook on low setting for 2 to 4 hours, keep on low to serve with chips and crackers.

CHEESE FONDUE

1 x can cheddar cheese soup
450 grams block processed cheese spread cut in 8 pieces
450 grams Swiss cheese, grated
1 x 350 ml. can beer (or apple cider)
½ teaspoon hot pepper sauce
drops liquid smoke flavouring

Place all ingredients in slow cooker. Stir to mix. Cover and cook on low setting for 2 hours. After 1 hour of cooking time, stir. Before serving, whisk to blend. Serve with bread sticks or vegetables for dipping.

CHEESY CAULIFLOWER AND BROCCOLI

285 grams cauliflower
285 grams broccoli
1 can cheddar cheese soup
4 slices bacon
salt and pepper to taste
25 grams grated cheddar cheese, if desired

Fry bacon until crisp; drain well on paper towels then crumble. Place broccoli and cauliflower in crockpot. Top with soup, sprinkle with bacon. Season with salt and pepper. Cover and cook on low setting for 4 to 5 hours. About 20 minutes before done, top with cheddar cheese if used. Serves 6 to 8.

CHILLI CON QUESO

2 tablespoons butter
1 medium onion, chopped
1 can jalapeno peppers, chopped
1 x 450 gram can tomatoes, chopped, un-drained
1 jar pimiento, chopped, drained
170 grams cheddar cheese, grated
salt and pepper, to taste

Sauté onion in butter in medium saucepan. Combine next 3 ingredients with onion. Heat to boiling, then allow to simmer for 10 to 15 minutes to meld the flavours. Add cheese, mixing thoroughly until melted. Serve immediately. Note: you can add browned minced beef or sausage if you'd like.

CHEESY CREAMED CORN

3 x 450 gram packets frozen corn
1 x 225 gram packet cream cheese
1 x 85 grams packet cream cheese
4 tablespoons butter
3 tablespoon water
3 tablespoons milk
2 tablespoons sugar
6 slices cheese

Combine all ingredients in crockpot, mix well. Cover and cook for 4 to 5 hours on low setting, or until heated through and cheese is melted. Stir well before serving.

CHEESE SOUFFLÉ

14 slices fresh white bread, crust removed
600 grams grated cheddar cheese
60 grams butter
6 large eggs
750 ml. milk, scalded
2 tablespoons Worcestershire sauce
½ teaspoon salt
paprika

Tear bread in small pieces. Place half in well greased crockpot. Add 115 grams cheese and half the butter. Add remaining bread, cheese and butter. Beat eggs, milk, Worcestershire sauce and salt. Pour over bread and cheese. Sprinkle with paprika. Cover and cook on low setting for 4 to 6 hours. Do not open until ready to serve.

CLASSIC CROCKPOT BAKED POTATOES

12 potatoes, more or less
foil for wrapping potatoes

Prick potatoes with fork and wrap each potato in foil. Fill dry crockpot with the wrapped potatoes. Cover and cook on LOW 8 to 10 hours, until potatoes are tender. Prick with a fork to check.

CONGRESSIONAL BEAN SOUP IN A CROCKPOT

450 grams small white beans
2 litres water
900 grams ham, diced
450 grams onion, diced
450 grams celery, chopped
2 tablespoons parsley, chopped
1 teaspoon salt
¼ teaspoon pepper
1 bay leaf

Assemble ingredients in slow cooker. Cover and cook on low setting for 8 to 10 hours or until beans are tender.

CLASSIC SWISS FONDUE

1 clove garlic
680 grams dry white wine
1 tablespoon lemon juice
450 grams Swiss cheese, grated
910 grams Cheddar cheese, grated
3 tablespoons flour
3 tablespoons kirsch
freshly ground nutmeg
pepper
paprika
1 loaf Italian or French bread, cut into 1-inch cubes

Rub an enamelled or stainless steel pan with garlic clove. Heat wine to a slow simmer (just under boiling). Add lemon juice. Combine cheeses and flour and gradually stir in. Using a figure-8 motion, stir constantly until cheese is melted. Pour into lightly greased crockpot. Add kirsch; stir well. Sprinkle with nutmeg, pepper and paprika. Cover and cook on high setting for 30 minutes, then turn to low setting for 2 to 5 hours. Keep on low setting while serving. Using fondue forks, dip bread cubes into fondue. Makes about 2 quarts

CORN CHOWDER

2 cans (450 grams) whole kernel corn, drained
2 to 3 medium potatoes, chopped
1 onion, chopped
½ teaspoon salt
pepper to taste
500 ml. chicken broth
500 ml. milk
60 grams flour or margarine

Combine first 6 ingredients in crockpot. Cover and cook on low setting for 7 to 9 hours. Purée in a blender or food processor, if desired, then return to pot. Stir in milk and butter; cook on high setting for about another hour. Serves 6 to 8.

CLASSIC CABBAGE ROLLS

1.5 litres water
12 large cabbage leaves
450 grams lean minced lamb
230 grams cooked rice
1 teaspoon salt
¼ teaspoon dried oregano leaves
¼ teaspoon ground nutmeg
¼ teaspoon black pepper
375 ml. tomato sauce

Bring water to the boil in large saucepan. Turn off heat. Soak cabbage leaves in water 5 minutes; remove, drain and cool. Combine lamb, rice, salt, oregano, nutmeg and pepper in large bowl. Place 2 tablespoonfuls mixture in center of each cabbage leaf; roll firmly. Place cabbage rolls in slow cooker, seam-side down. Pour tomato sauce over cabbage rolls. Cover and cook on low setting for 8 to 10 hours.

COCONUT CREAM OF MUSHROOM SOUP

250 ml. boiling water
680 grams fresh mushrooms, trimmed and sliced
2 onions, finely chopped
4 garlic cloves, crushed
½ teaspoon dried thyme leaves or 2 sprigs fresh thyme
1 teaspoon sea salt
½ teaspoon black peppercorns (cracked)
1 bay leaf
1 litre vegetable broth or beef broth
250 ml. coconut milk
4 tablespoons virgin coconut oil

In a heatproof bowl, soak half of the mushrooms in boiling water for 30 minutes. Drain through a fine sieve, reserving liquid. Pat mushrooms dry with paper towel and chop finely and set aside. In a frying pan heat 1 tablespoon virgin coconut oil over medium heat. Add fresh mushrooms, cook (stirring until they lose their liquid)and transfer to crockpot. In same pan, melt remaining 3 tablespoons virgin coconut oil. Add onions and cook, stirring until softened. Add reserved mushrooms, garlic, thyme, salt and peppercorns and cook, stirring, for 1 minute. Transfer to slow cooker. Add bay leaf, broth, coconut milk and reserved mushroom soaking liquid and stir to combine. Cover and cook on low setting for 6 to 8 hours or on high setting for 3 to 4 hours. Discard bay leaf. Serves 6 to 8.

CREAMY CHEESE SCALLOPED POTATOES

2 tablespoons dried minced onion
1 medium clove garlic, crushed and finely minced
1 teaspoon salt
8 to 10 medium potatoes, sliced
1 packet cream cheese, cubed
½ cup shredded cheddar cheese (optional)

Spray slow cooker with non-stick butter flavour cooking spray. In a small bowl or cup, combine onion, garlic, salt, and pepper. Layer about ¼ of the sliced potatoes in the bottom of a slow cooker. Sprinkle with about ¼ of the onion and garlic mixture. Layer with about 1/3 of the cream cheese cubes. Repeat layers, ending with seasonings. Cover and cook on high setting for 3 to 4 hours, until potatoes are tender. In last 20 to 30 minutes of cooking, stir potatoes to distribute cream cheese. Potatoes can be partially mashed at this point. If desired, top with ½ cup of shredded mild Cheddar cheese. Cover and continue to cook, about 10 minutes, just until melted. Serve when potatoes are tender. Serves 6.

CREAM OF SWEET POTATO SOUP

3 sweet potatoes, peeled and sliced
500 ml. chicken stock
1 teaspoon sugar
1/8 teaspoon each ground cloves and nutmeg
salt to taste
325 ml. light cream, single cream, or milk

Put sweet potatoes and stock in cooker. Cover and cook on high setting for 2 to 3 hours or until potatoes are tender. Force potatoes and liquid through food mill or purée in blender. Put back in cooker with remaining ingredients. Cover and cook on high setting for 1 to 2 hours. Serve hot or chilled with a dollop of sour cream if desired. Makes about a litre.

CREAMY CORN

160 grams corn
2 tablespoons sugar
2 eggs
30 grams flour
2 tablespoons butter
250 ml. milk
½ teaspoon salt

Mix corn, sugar, eggs, flour, butter, milk and salt; place in slow cooker. Cook on high setting for one hour.

CREAMY LENTIL AND MUSHROOM SOUP

225 grams dry lentils
2 medium carrots, sliced ¼ inch thick
1 medium onion, chopped
3 cloves garlic, minced
225 grams cup mushrooms, sliced
1 cup sliced celery snipped parsley
4 cups water
1 x can condensed cream of mushroom soup
2 teaspoons instant vegetable stock granules
(or 2 cubes)

sour cream

In a saucepan, sauté onions, mushrooms, garlic, and celery till just slightly browned, about 10 minutes. In a large crockpot, combine the lentils, carrots, onion, garlic, mushrooms, celery and parsley. Stir in water, mushroom soup, and stock cubes/granules. Cover; cook on low setting for 10 to 12 hours or high setting for 5 to 6 hours. Top each serving with a dollop of sour cream. Makes 4 servings.

CREAMY SPINACH DIP

225 grams cream cheese, cubed
140 grams frozen chopped spinach
2 tablespoons pimento, diced
1 teaspoon Worcestershire sauce
1/4 teaspoon garlic salt
60 ml single cream
2 tablespoons parmesan cheese, grated
2 teaspoons onion, finely chopped
½ teaspoon thyme

Combine cream cheese and cream in crockpot. cover and heat until cheese is melted (30 to 60 minutes). Add remaining ingredients, cover and heat for a further 30 minutes. Serve with raw vegetables, crackers, or bread pieces.

CREAMY RED POTATOES

910 grams small red potatoes, quartered
2 x 225 gram packets cream cheese, softened
1 can cream of potato soup, undiluted
salad dressing to your taste

Place potatoes in crockpot. In a small bowl, beat cream cheese, soup and salad dressing, mix. Stir into potatoes. Cover and cook on low setting for 8 hours or until potatoes are tender. Also add about a tablespoon of milk.

CREAMY SPINACH NOODLE CASSEROLE

225 grams dry spinach noodles
2 tablespoon. vegetable oil
350 ml. sour cream
30 grams plain flour
225 grams cottage cheese
4 green onions, finely-chopped
2 teaspoons Worcestershire sauce
1 dash hot pepper sauce
2 teaspoons garlic salt

This tasty side dish makes approximately 5 servings. Cook noodles in a pot of salted, boiling water until just tender. Drain and rinse with cold water. Toss with vegetable oil. Combine sour cream and flour in a large bowl, mixing well. Stir in cottage cheese, green onions, Worcestershire sauce, hot pepper sauce and garlic salt. Fold noodles into mixture until well combined. Generously grease the inside of a slow cooker and pour in noodle mixture. Cover and cook on high setting for 1½ to 2 hours.

CREOLE BLACK BEANS

900 grams smoked sausage, cut into 1 inch slices
3 x 425 gram cans black beans, drained
325 grams onions, chopped
325 grams green pepper, chopped
325 grams celery, chopped
3 cloves garlic, crushed
2 teaspoons leaf thyme
1½ teaspoons leaf oregano
1½ teaspoons white pepper
¼ teaspoon black pepper
¼ teaspoon cayenne pepper
1 chicken stock cube
5 bay leaves
1 can tomato sauce
250 ml. water
hot boiled rice

Brown sausage in a frying pan over medium heat. Drain fat and transfer to crockpot. Combine remaining ingredients in crockpot. Cover and cook on low setting for 8 hours, or on high setting for 4 hours. Remove bay leaves. Serve over cooked rice. Serves 6 to 8.

CROCK-ROASTED SUMMER VEGETABLES

2 large red bell peppers, seeded and cut into strips
2 large red onions, cut into 8 wedges each
3 medium yellow squash, ends trimmed and sliced ½ inch thick
3 medium zucchinis, ends trimmed and cut into thick matchsticks
145 grams fresh green beans, stem end snapped off
4 garlic cloves, peeled
2 to 3 tablespoons olive oil
1 tablespoon chopped fresh basil or savory
salt
fresh ground pepper
3 tablespoons flat leaf parsley
2-4 tablespoons white balsamic vinegar or dark balsamic vinegar

Add all the vegetables to the slow cooker; add in the oil and basil. Season with salt and pepper to taste; toss to coat evenly. Cover and cook on high setting for 1½ to 2 hours or until the vegetables are just tender and still hold their shape. Serve sprinkled with the parsley and vinegar. Serves 6.

CROCKPOT ARTICHOKES

5 artichokes, remove stalks and tough leaves
1½ teaspoon salt
8 peppercorns
2 stalks celery, cut up
½ lemon, sliced
500 ml. boiling water

Combine all ingredients in crockpot. Cook on high setting for 4 to 5 hours.

CROCKPOT GERMAN POTATO SALAD

1.5 kilos sliced potatoes
230 grams onions, chopped
230 grams celery, sliced
60 grams green peppers, diced
65 ml vinegar
2 to 3 tablespoons sugar
65 ml. oil
chopped parsley
sliced bacon, cooked and crumbled sugar,
optional

Combine all ingredients except parsley and bacon. Add salt and pepper to taste. Stir and cook for 5 to 7 hours in crockpot. Garnish with bacon and parsley. Place all ingredients in cooker. Toss gently. Cover and cook on low setting for about 4 hours. Makes about 3 litres.

CROCKPOT SQUASH

2 squashes, cut in half and seeded
1¼ teaspoons salt
¼ teaspoon pepper
½ cup water
4 tablespoons butter
1 heaped tablespoon brown sugar
2 slices bacon, diced

Season squashes with salt and pepper. Sprinkle with remaining ingredients. Pour water into slow cooker. Add squashes to the crockpot, arranging so they do not rest directly on top of each other. Cook on high setting for 1 hour. Reduce to low setting and cook for about 6 hours longer, until tender.

CURRY-SPICED LENTILS AND SPINACH

1½ teaspoons curry powder
½ teaspoon ground cumin
1 teaspoon ginger
¼ teaspoon turmeric
¼ teaspoon cayenne
1 medium onion, chopped
2 cloves garlic, crushed and minced
1 cup lentils, rinsed
¼ cup converted rice
1 packet chopped spinach or other greens
1 can vegetable or chicken broth
salt to taste
chopped tomato and mint for garnish, if
desired

Combine first 11 ingredients in the slow cooker. Cover and cook on low setting for about 6 hours, or until rice and lentils are tender but not mushy. Add salt to taste; serve garnished with chopped tomato and mint if desired.

EASY CROCKPOT VEGETABLES

2 x 453 gram bags of your favourite frozen
vegetables
1 can condensed cream of celery soup or
cream of mushroom soup
seasoned salt
parsley
pepper
crushed garlic or garlic powder

Take two frozen bags of vegetables and a can of cream of celery soup, throw in some parsley and salt seasoned, and pepper a little garlic. Good results guaranteed!. Cook on high setting for 1 hour or on low setting for 2 hours.

EASY SPLIT PEA SOUP

450 grams dried split peas
450 grams diced fully cooked lean ham
225 grams diced carrots
1 medium onion, chopped
2 garlic cloves, crushed
2 bay leaves
½ teaspoon salt
½ teaspoon pepper
1.25 litres boiling water
250 ml. hot milk

In a slow cooker, layer the first nine ingredients in order listed (do not stir). Cover and cook on high setting for 4 to 5 hours or until vegetables are tender. Stir in milk. Discard bay leaves before serving. Serves 9.

EGGPLANT PARMIGIANA

4 large eggplants
2 eggs
80 ml. water
3 tablespoons flour
85 grams seasoned bread crumbs
120 grams parmesan cheese
1 large can tomato sauce
450 grams mozzarella cheese, sliced
extra virgin olive oil

Pare eggplant and cut in ½ inch slices; place in bowl in layers and sprinkle each layer with salt and allow to stand 30 minutes to drain excess water; dry on paper towels. Mix egg with water and flour. Dip eggplant slices in mixture, drain slightly. Sauté a few slices at a time quickly in hot olive oil. Combine seasoned breadcrumbs with the Parmesan cheese. In removable liner, layer a quarter of the eggplant, top with a quarter of the crumbs, a quarter of the tomato sauce and a quarter of the mozzarella cheese. Repeat three times to make four layers of eggplant, crumbs, sauce and mozzarella cheese. Place liner in base. Cover and cook on low setting for 4 to 5 hours or on auto for about 3 hours.

GERMAN POTATO SALAD

2 potatoes, sliced
115 grams onions, chopped
115 grams celery sliced
60 grams. green peppers, diced
60 ml. vinegar
60 ml. oil
chopped parsley
sliced bacon, cooked and crumbled

Combine all ingredients except parsley and bacon. Add salt and pepper to taste. Stir and cook for 5 to 6 hours in slow cooker. Add sugar if needed. Garnish with bacon and parsley.

GREEN BEAN AND POTATO CASSEROLE

900 grams fresh trimmed and cut green beans
4 to 6 medium red-skinned potatoes, sliced about ¼ inch thick
1 large onion, sliced
1 teaspoon dried dill weed
1 teaspoon salt
1/2 teaspoon pepper
1 can cream of chicken soup, undiluted
margarine

Spray the crockpot with cooking spray or lightly grease with butter or margarine. Layer sliced potatoes, sliced onion and green beans, sprinkling with dill and salt and pepper as you go. Dot with margarine, about 1 tablespoon total, and add about 2 tablespoons of water. Cover and cook on high setting for 4 hours or on low setting for about 8 hours. Stir in soup or sauce; turn to low setting and cook an additional 30 minutes or leave on low until serving time or up to 4 hours. Serves 6 to 8. Note: Add bits of cooked bacon for extra flavour.

HARVARD BEETROOT

110 grams granulated sugar
2 tablespoons flour
65 ml. water
65 ml. cider vinegar
2 cans whole beets, drained

Mix sugar and flour and stir in the water and vinegar. Place beets in slow cooker; stir in vinegar and sugar mixture. Cover and cook on high setting for 3 to 4 hours. 4 to 6 servings

HOT ARTICHOKE DIP

170 grams artichoke hearts, marinated
80 ml. mayonnaise
1 tablespoon pimento, diced (optional)
120 grams parmesan cheese, grated
80 ml. sour cream
1/8 teaspoon garlic powder

Drain and chop artichoke hearts. Combine all ingredients and place in crockpot. Cover and heat on high setting for 30 to 60 minutes until hot. Serve with tortilla chips or assorted crackers.

HOT BROCCOLI DIP

285 grams chopped broccoli
113 grams margarine
1 medium onion, chopped
1 can cream of mushroom soup
200 grams cheese, cut up
70 grams mushroom pieces

Combine first 3 ingredients in a Sauté pan and cook until onions are clear. Transfer to the slow cooker. Add soup, cheese, and mushrooms, heat on low for about 1½ to 2 hours, or until cheese is melted and mixture is hot. Dip with large corn chips or can be poured over baked potatoes. Freezes well.

HOT CHILI CON QUESO

350 ml. single cream, scalded
460 grams grated cheese
1 tablespoon butter
1/2 onion, minced
1 medium clove garlic, crushed
60 ml. dry white wine or low-sodium stock
30 grams flour
60 ml. water
115 grams chopped green chilli peppers
1 to 2 tablespoons chopped jalapeno
salt and pepper
dash cayenne pepper

Pour scalded single cream into buttered crockpot. Turn to high seting and stir in cheeses. In small frying pan, sauté onion and garlic in butter until onion is tender. Add wine or stock and stir well. Add to cheese mixture. Combine flour with water and stir in. Cook covered on high setting for 30 minutes, or until cheese begins to melt. Turn to low setting and cook for about 4 to 6 hours, stirring 2 or 3 times during the first hour and occasionally after that. If the mixture is too thin, mix 2 tablespoons of flour with 2 tablespoons of water and add. Serve warm with tortilla chips and/or other dippers.

HOT GERMAN POTATO SALAD

5 medium potatoes, cut into ¼ inch slices
1 large onion, chopped
85 ml. water
85 ml. cider vinegar
2 tablespoons all-purpose flour
2 tablespoons sugar
1 teaspoon salt
½ teaspoon celery seeds
¼ teaspoon pepper
4 slices crisp cooked bacon, crumbled

Mix potatoes and onion in a large slow cooker. Mix remaining ingredients except bacon; pour into cooker. Caver and cook on low setting for 8 to 10 hours or until potatoes are tender. Stir in bacon. Serves 6.

101

HOT SPINACH DIP

2 x 285 gram packets frozen chopped
spinach
1 large jar jalapeno cheese sauce
1 can cream of mushroom soup
1 x 85 grams packet cream cheese
2 tablespoon dried minced onion

Thaw spinach completely. Drain, and squeeze as much moisture as possible from spinach. Combine all ingredients in the slow cooker and cook on low setting for about 2 hours, until hot (stir a few times to blend well). Keep warm in crockpot. Serve with corn chips or crackers.

ITALIAN GREEN BEANS

910 grams sweet Italian sausage
1 x 425 gram can stewed tomatoes, chopped
4 x 225 gram cans sliced mushrooms (do not
drain)
¼-½ teaspoon onion and/or garlic powders
½ teaspoon basil and/or oregano
3 x 450 gram cans Italian style green beans,
2 of them drained
120 grams Parmesan cheese

Brown sausage and drain. Add all ingredients except green beans. Mix thoroughly and simmer for 15 minutes. Add green beans and mix. Bake in a slow cooker on low setting for up to 3 hours.

ITALIAN ZUCCHINI

450 grams zucchini, sliced, unpeeled
1 large onion , chopped
3 large tomatoes, chopped
65 ml. Italian salad dressing
2 tablespoons sugar

Spray a slow cooker container with olive oil-flavored cooking spray. In prepared container, combine zucchini and onion. Add undrained tomatoes, Italian dressing, and sugar (or low-fat equivalent). Mix well to combine. Cover and cook on low setting for 4 to 6 hours. Mix well before serving.   Serves 6.

MACARONI CHEESE

1 x 450 gram packet macaroni, cooked and
drained
1 tablespoon salad oil
1 can evaporated milk
375 ml. milk
1 teaspoon salt
600 grams grated mature cheddar cheese
115 grams melted butter

Lightly grease crockpot. Toss macaroni and oil. Add all remaining ingredients. Stir, cover and cook on low setting for 3 to 4 hours, stirring occasionally.

MACARONI PIE

225 grams packet macaroni, cooked
600 grams. grated cheese
1 can of evaporated milk
375 ml. milk
2 eggs
60 grams. margarine
1 teaspoon sugar
salt and pepper to taste

Combine cooked macaroni with other ingredients and pour into a greased crockpot. Cook for 3½ hours on medium heat.

MAPLE GLAZED SWEET POTATOES

5 medium sweet potatoes
60 grams brown sugar
60 ml. pure maple syrup
60 ml. apple cider
dash salt and pepper to taste

Peel sweet potatoes and cut into ¼ to ½ inch thick slices; place in crockpot. Whisk remaining ingredients together and pour over potatoes. Cover and cook on low setting for 7 to 9 hours. Stir a few times, if possible, to keep them coated. Serves 4.

MARMALADE-GLAZED CARROTS

1 x 900 gram packet fresh baby carrots
120 ml. marmalade
1 tablespoon water
2 tablespoon brown sugar
1 tablespoon butter
½ teaspoon cinnamon
¼ teaspoon nutmeg
1 tablespoons cornflour
2 tablespoons water
salt and pepper to taste

Combine all ingredients in crockpot and cook on low setting for 7 to 9 hours, until carrots are tender. About 15 minutes before serving, make a paste of the cornflour and cold water; stir into carrots. Taste and adjust seasonings. Serves 4 to 6 as a side dish.

MEXICAN CHEESE DIP

230 grams cheese
1 teaspoon taco seasoning (optional)
½ can tomatoes with chilies

Cube cheese and place in crockpot. Cover and heat for 30 to 60 minutes, until melted, stirring occasionally. Stir in tomatoes and seasoning.

Cover and continue heating for a further 30 minutes. Serve with tortilla chips or corn chips.

MIXED VEGETABLE BAKE

2 x 480 gram cans creamed corn
2 x 450 gram cans green beans
2 x 450 gram cans peas
1 x 480 gram can tomatoes
120 ml. mayonnaise
1 teaspoon tarragon
1 teaspoon basil
½ teaspoon salt
pepper

Combine all ingredients in removable liner, mix well to blend herbs. Place liner in base. Cover and cook on low setting for 4-6 hours.

ORANGE GLAZED CARROTS

600 grams thinly sliced carrots
3 tablespoons butter or margarine
500 ml. water
3 tablespoons orange marmalade
¼ teaspoon salt
2 tablespoons chopped pecans

Combine carrots, water, and salt in crockpot. Cover and cook on high setting for 2 to 3 hours or until the carrots are done. Drain well; stir in remaining ingredients. Cover and cook on high setting for a further 20 to 30 minutes. Makes 5 to 6 servings.

PAPRIKOSH

5 large carrots (cubed)
8 large potatoes, cubed
5 large celery stalks
2 large onions (sliced thin)
3 tablespoons paprika
salt and pepper to taste

Throw all ingredients into the slow cooker, and add water to cover vegetables. Cook on high setting for 4 hours.

PARMESAN SCALLOPED POTATOES

5 to 6 red potatoes, sliced
6 slices turkey bacon or other smoked meat
3 ounces freshly grated parmesan cheese
1 can condensed cream of mushroom soup
salt and pepper to taste

Layer all ingredients in lightly buttered crockpot. Cover and cook on low setting for 7 to 9 hours. Adjust seasonings. Serves 4.

PARTY MIX

1.4 kg. assorted cereals (oat, rice, wheat in various shapes)
150 grams peanuts, pecans, cashews, or mixed nuts
225 grams mini pretzel sticks
120 grams butter or margarine, melted
4 tablespoons Worcestershire sauce
dash hot pepper sauce
½ teaspoon seasoned salt
½ teaspoon garlic salt
½ teaspoon onion salt

Combine cereals, nuts and pretzels in crockpot. Mix melted butter with remaining ingredients

and pour over the cereal mixture, tossing to coat. Cook uncovered on high setting for 2 hours, stirring about every 30 minutes. Turn to low setting and cook for another 2 to 6 hours. Store in an airtight container. Makes about 10 cups.

PASTA AND BROCCOLI

1 medium onion
1 can cream of mushroom soup
450 grams. cheese
1 packet frozen broccoli and cauliflower
1 packet shell noodles

Mix onion, cream of mushroom soup and cheese in a slow cooker on high setting until melted. Add broccoli and cauliflower until hot. Add cooked shells right before serving.

PIZZA DIP

1 large cream cheese softened
1 jar pizza sauce
1 small can chopped olives
1 medium onion chopped
1 packet sliced pepperoni
1 packet grated cheese for pizza

Spread cream cheese in bottom of slow cooker. Then mix up the pizza sauce, onion, olives and pepperoni and spread on top of the cream cheese. Sprinkle with the pizza cheese and cook on low setting until the cheese on top melts. Serve with tortilla chips. You could add other pizza toppings to this or delete some that are listed.

POTATO AND CAULIFLOWER DAL WITH SPICY SHALLOTS

1 cup yellow split peas, soaked overnight, drained and rinsed .
2 tablespoons clarified butter or vegetable oil
2 onions, finely chopped
4 stalks celery, peeled and thinly sliced
4 garlic cloves, minced
1 tablespoon grated gingerroot
1 teaspoon curry powder
1 teaspoon salt
½ teaspoon black pepper
¼ teaspoon ground nutmeg
3 cups vegetable broth or water
3 potatoes, peeled and cut into 1/2-inch cubes
1 small cauliflower, cut into florets or 4 cups frozen cauliflower, thawed
Spicy Shallots (see below *)
2 tablespoons vegetable oil
2 long french shallots, thinly sliced or 8 green onions, white part only thinly sliced
¼ - ½ teaspoon finely chopped chili peppers
1 tablespoon finely chopped cilantro
2 tablespoons balsamic vinegar or lemon juice

In a frying pan, heat clarified butter or oil over medium heat. Add onions and celery and cook until softened. Add garlic, gingerroot, curry powder, salt, pepper and nutmeg and cook, stirring, for 1 minute. Add vegetable broth or water and bring to the boil. Place potatoes, cauliflower and soaked peas in slow cooker. Pour onion and celery and spice mixture over and stir well. Cover and cook on low setting for 8 to 10 hours or on high setting for 4 to 5 hours, until vegetables are tender.

* To make Spicy Shallots: In a frying pan, heat clarified butter or oil over medium high heat. Add shallots and cook, stirring, until crisp. Remove pan from heat. Stir in chilies, cilantro and balsamic vinegar or lemon juice. Transfer to a small bowl. Ladle potato and cauliflower Dal into individual bowls, top with Spicy Shallots and stir well. Serves 6 to 8.

POTATO CASSEROLE

1 packet frozen hash browns
1 small carton ranch dip
1 can cream of potato soup
salt, pepper
dried onions to taste
140 grams grated cheddar cheese

Mix first four ingredients. Put into slow cooker. Place grated cheese on top, and cook on high setting for about 4 hours. You could probably add ham or other meat, for a complete meal in one.

POTATOES PERFECT

115 grams bacon, diced
2 medium onions, thinly sliced
4 medium potatoes, thinly sliced
230 grams cheddar cheese, thinly sliceed
salt and pepper, to taste
butter

Line crockpot with aluminium foil, leaving enough to overlap potatoes when finished. Layer half each of the bacon, onions, potatoes and cheese in slow cooker. Season to taste and dot with butter. Repeat layers of bacon, onions, potatoes and cheese. Dot with butter. Overlap with remaining foil. Cover and cook on low setting for 10 to 12 hours.

POTATO SOUP

6-8 potatoes, chunked
2 medium carrots, cubed
2 stalks celery, cubed
1 medium onion, chopped
1 tablespoon. parsley flakes
1.25 litres
salt and pepper to taste

Cook in crockpot on low setting for 8 hours or until vegetables are cooked. One hour before serving, add one can of evaporated milk.

POTATOES WITH LEEKS

500 grams potatoes, sliced
2 medium parsnips, peeled and sliced
2 medium leeks
1 cup milk
1 pound cabbage
½ teaspoon mace or ¼ teaspoon nutmeg
2 small cloves garlic, crushed
1 dash salt
1 dash pepper
2 tablespoons butter
parsley

Cook the potatoes and parsnips in water until tender. While vegetables are cooking, chop leeks (light green as well as whites) and simmer in the milk until soft. Next, cook the cabbage and have warm and well chopped. Drain the potatoes and parsnips and season with mace, garlic, salt and pepper; beat well. Add the cooked leeks and milk (be careful not to break down the leeks too much). Finally, blend in the cooked chopped cabbage and butter. The texture should be that of a smooth-buttery potato with well distributed pieces of leek and cabbage. Garnish with fresh minced parsley. This recipe can also be made by layering the vegetables (first, cook cabbage just until tender), starting with potatoes, in a slow cooker, then cooking for 7 to 9 hours, until vegetables are tender. Drain vegetables and blend with milk and butter as above and garnish with parsley. Serves 6.

REFRIED BEAN DIP

1 x 560 gram can refried beans
¼ teaspoon salt
125 grams grated cheddar cheese
1 x 115 gram can chopped green chillis
2 tablespoons bottled taco sauce
120 grams chopped green onions
tortilla chips

In crockpot combine beans with cheese, chillis, onions, salt, and taco sauce. Cover and cook on low setting for 2 to 2½ hours. Serve hot from the pot.

ROASTED VEGETABLE TRIO POT

600 grams sliced raw potatoes
600 grams sliced carrots
1 x 425 gram can beef broth
120 grams chopped onions

In a slow cooker, combine potatoes, carrots and onion. Pour beef broth evenly over top. Cover and cook on high setting for 4 to 6 hours. Mix well before serving.

SAVOURY SALSA-CORN CAKE

2 x 225 gram boxes corn muffin mix
1 x 425 gram can creamed corn
2 eggs
120 ml. sour cream
1 x 115 gram can chopped green chillis (do not drain)
2 tablespoons soft margarine
3 to 4 tablespoons chunky salsa

In a medium bowl, combine creamed corn, eggs, sour cream, chillis, and margarine. Whisk together until well combined. Add corn muffin mix, stirring well to combine. Generously grease a large slow cooker with margarine or butter. Pour batter into the slow cooker. Spoon salsa over the top and cut into the batter. Cover and cook on high setting for about 2 ½ hours. Turn heat off and let cool with lid ajar, for about 15 minutes. Loosen sides with a knife and invert onto a large plate. If a little of the top sticks to the bottom of the pot, dollop a little salsa on the top, or decorate with sour cream and chopped green onion. Delicious side dish! Serves 6 to 8.

SCALLOPED CORN

3 large eggs
250 ml. single cream
1 tablespoon sugar
1/4 teaspoon salt
1/4 teaspoon pepper
3 to 4 tablespoons minced onion
1 x 160 gram packet frozen creamed corn, thawed
120 grams coarsely crushed cracker crumbs

Wisk milk and eggs together, then mix in remaining ingredients. Pour into lightly buttered casserole which will fit in the slow cooker. Cover and cook on high for 2 ½ hours, or until knife inserted in center comes out clean. Serves 6 as a side dish.

SIMMERED CABBAGE AND TOMATOES

4 tablespoons butter
1 medium sweet onion, coarsely chopped
1 x 794 gram can crushed tomatoes
1 tablespoon cider vinegar
¾ teaspoon sugar
2 or 3 garlic cloves, crushed
½ -1 teaspoon salt
¼ teaspoon pepper
¼ teaspoon oregano
¼ - ½ teaspoon celery seeds
1 head green cabbage, coarsely chopped
8 ounces cream cheese, cut into cubes

Put everything in the crockpot EXCEPT the cream cheese. Cook on low setting for 6 to 8 hours or on high setting for about 3 hours (depends on how tender you like your cabbage). When cooked, stir in the cream cheese. Serves 8.

SCALLOPED POTATO-TOMATO POT

900 grams frozen grated hash browns
1 x 450 gram can cut green beans, rinsed and drained
60 grams finely chopped onion
1 teaspoon dried parsley flakes
1 x 300 gram can cream of celery soup
1 x 410 gram can stewed tomatoes (do not drain)

In a slow cooker, combine hash browns, green beans and onion. In a medium bowl, combine parsley flakes, celery soup and un-drained stewed tomatoes. Add soup mixture to potato mixture, and mix well to combine. Cover and cook on low setting for 6 to 8 hours. Mix well before serving.

SLOW-COOKED BROCCOLI

600 grams broccoli
1 x 300 gram can condensed cream of celery soup, undiluted
150 grams mature cheddar cheese, grated and divided
60 grams chopped onion
½ teaspoon Worcestershire sauce
¼ teaspoon pepper
120 grams crushed butter-flavoured crackers(about 25)
2 tablespoons butter or margarine

In a large bowl, combine broccoli, soup, 125 grams cheese, onion, Worcestershire sauce and pepper. Pour into a greased slow cooker. Sprinkle crackers on top; dot with butter. Cover and cook on high setting for 2½ to 3 hours. Sprinkle with remaining cheese. Cook 10 minutes longer or until the cheese is melted. Yield: 8-10 servings.

SCALLOPED POTATOES

10 large potatoes, thinly sliced
2 large onions, chopped
2 cans condensed cheddar cheese soup
250 ml. milk

In a small bowl, combine soup with milk. In removable liner, layer one half of the potatoes and one half of the chopped onions; spread one half of the soup-milk mixture. Repeat layering using rest of ingredients. Place in base. Cover and cook on low setting for 6 to 8 hours, on high setting for 3 to 4 hours or on auto for 5 hours.

SIMPLE SAUCY POTATOES

4 x 425 gram cans sliced white potatoes, drained
2 cans condensed cream of celery soup, undiluted
500 ml. sour cream
10 bacon strips, cooked and crumbled
6 green onions , thinly sliced

Place potatoes in slow cooker. Combine the remaining ingredients; pour over the potatoes and mix well. Cover and cook on high setting for 4 to 5 hours.

SLOW-COOKED CORN PUDDING

60 grams chopped onion
60 grams chopped green pepper
60 grams chopped fresh tomato
1 can cream-style corn
4 large eggs
120 ml. evaporated milk
½ teaspoon salt
¼ teaspoon pepper

Sauté onion and green pepper until slightly softened; add tomato and sauté for 1 minute more. In a medium-sized bowl, whisk together the eggs, milk, creamed corn and seasonings; add the sautéed vegetables. Lightly grease a large crockpot (or a soufflé dish which fits in a larger crockpot) and pour the mixture in. Cook on high setting for 2½ to 3 hours; add grated cheese to the top and cook until cheese is melted.

SPLIT PEA AND HAM SOUP

450 grams dried green split peas, rinsed
1 hambone or 500 grams diced ham
3 carrots, peeled & sliced
1 medium onion, chopped
2 stalks of celery plus leaves, chopped
1 or 2 cloves of garlic, crushed
1 bay leaf
60 grams. fresh parsley, chopped (optional)
1 tablespoon. seasoned salt (or to taste)
½ teaspoon fresh pepper
2.4 litres hot water

Layer ingredients in slow cooker, pour in water. DO NOT STIR. Cover and cook on high setting for 4 to 5 hours or on low setting for 8 to 10 hours until peas are very soft and ham falls off bone. Remove bones and bay leaf. Serve garnished with croutons. Freezes well.

SLOW-COOKER CREAMY CORN

1 large bag frozen corn
1 x 225 gram packet cream cheese
115 grams margarine
salt and pepper to taste

Melt cream cheese and margarine in microwave. Spray slow cooker with vegetable spray. Put melted cream cheese and margarine in slow cooker. Add corn, salt and pepper. Cook in slow cooker for two hours on low setting .

SOUTHERN STYLE GREEN BEAN & POTATO CASSEROLE

4 to 6 medium red potatoes, sliced about ¼ inch thick (peeled or not)
1 kg. whole fresh green beans, trimmed
6 slices bacon, diced fried and drained
2 tablespoons minced dried onion
1 can cream of celery soup
salt and pepper to taste

Place sliced potatoes and green beans in slow cooker, and add other ingredients. Cover and cook on low setting for 7 to 9 hours. Serves 4 to 6.

SPINACH SOUFFLE

900 grams frozen spinach, thawed and drained
60 grams grated onion
1 x 225 gram packet light cream cheese, softened
120 ml. mayonnaise
120 grams grated cheddar cheese
2 eggs, beaten
1/4 teaspoon white or black pepper
dash nutmeg

Mix thawed and drained spinach together with onion. Beat remaining ingredients and blend in spinach mixture. Spoon mixture into a large, lightly buttered crockpot (or soufflé dish to fit in a larger crockpot) and cook on high setting for 2 to 3 hours.

SPINACH ARTICHOKE DIP

1 can artichoke hearts, drained and chopped
2 bunches of fresh spinach (about 450 grams)
450 grams cream cheese, cubed
250 grams cheddar cheese, cubed
250 grams mozzarella cheese, cubed
3 garlic cloves, crushed
¼ teaspoon black pepper

Cube cheese and add to slow cooker. Chop artichoke hearts and spinach and add to cheese. Place in a slow cooker, and add garlic and pepper. Heat on high setting, until melted, stirring occasionally. Takes about 1 to 2 hours.

STUFFED GREEN PEPPERS

1 x 285 gram packet frozen corn kernels
1 x 425 gram can red kidney beans drained and rinsed
1 x 300 gram can diced tomatoes
60 ml. salsa
60 grams chopped onions
300 grams cooked rice
1 teaspoon Worcestershire sauce
¼ teaspoon salt
½ teaspoon pepper
160 grams grated Cheddar cheese, divided
6 green peppers. tops removed and seeded

Combine all ingredients, except 60 grams cheese and green peppers. Stuff peppers. Arrange peppers in crockpot. Cover and cook on low setting for 6 to 8 hours (or on high setting for 3 to 4 hours). Sprinkle with 60 grams cheese during the last 30 minutes. Makes 6 servings.

SQUASH CASSEROLE

5 cups yellow squash, canned or frozen
120 grams butter or margarine, melted
1 can cream of chicken soup
2 slices cubed bread
250 ml. sour cream

Place squash in slow cooker with butter and cook for 1 hour. Add soup as it comes from the can, and cook until hot. Add bread and sour cream and cook until bubbly.

STUFFED POTATOES

6 baking potatoes, washed
3 tablespoons butter
250 ml. milk
chopped chives
1 teaspoon salt
1/8 teaspoon pepper
3 tablespoons Parmesan cheese
grated cheddar cheese

Place damp potatoes in bottom of slow cooker. Cover and cook on low setting for 6 to 8 hours. Remove and cut a slice, lengthwise, from each potato. Scoop out insides. Save shell. Add remaining ingredients and beat until fluffy. Spoon mixture back into shells and top each with grated cheddar cheese. Bake at 425°F for 15 minutes or until cheese is melted and bubbly. Serves 6.

STEWED TOMATOES

6 to 8 ripe tomatoes
2 tablespoons margarine
1 medium onion, thinly sliced
165 grams chopped celery
120 grams chopped green pepper
3 tablespoons sugar (more or less)
1 small bay leaf
1 teaspoon salt
1/8 teaspoon pepper

Core tomatoes; place in boiling water for about 15 to 20 seconds, then into ice water to cool quickly; peel. Cut tomatoes in wedges. In crockpot, combine all ingredients. Cover and cook on low setting for 8 to 9 hours. Remove bay leaf. Sprinkle top with parsley, if desired. Serve as a side dish or freeze in portions for soups or other recipes. Serves 6.

SUN-DRIED TOMATO SPAGHETTI SAUCE

300 grams chopped sun-dried tomatoes
1 medium onion, chopped
150 grams celery, chopped
2 cloves garlic, crushed
1 large can whole or chopped tomatoes (do not drain)
170 grams dry white wine
1 teaspoon dried fennel seed
1½ teaspoon basil
½ teaspoon oregano
½ teaspoon pepper
Salt to taste

Place all ingredients in Crockpot and cook on low for 6-8 hours. Note: You can add mushrooms if desired.

SUNSHINE SQUASH

1 butternut squash, about 900 grams, peeled, seeded and diced
1 large can tomatoes (do not drain)
1 can corn, drained
1 medium onion, coarsely chopped
1 clove garlic, crushed well
1 green bell pepper, seeded and cut into 1 inch pieces
1 can green chillis, coarsely chopped
120 ml. chicken broth
1/2 teaspoon salt
¼ teaspoon black pepper
1 tablespoon plus 1½ teaspoons tomato paste

Combine all ingredients except tomato paste in slow cooker. Cover and cook on low setting for 6 hours or until squash is tender. Remove about ¼ of a cup of cooking liquid and blend with tomato paste. Stir into slow-cooker. Cook for 30 minutes or until mixture is slightly thickened and heated through. Serves 6- 8.

VEGETABLE CASSEROLE

160 grams carrots, cut in strips, cooked and drained
160 grams celery, diced
1 onion
60 grams green pepper, diced
500 ml. tomato juice
650 grams green beans, drained
1 teaspoon salt
dash of pepper
3 tablespoons tapioca
1 tablespoon sugar

Mix all ingredients together in a slow cooker. Dot with 2 tablespoons margarine and cook on low setting for 8 to 10 hours or on high setting for 4 to 5 hours.

SWISS CHEESE SCALLOPED POTATOES

900 grams baking potatoes, peeled and thinly sliced
120 grams finely chopped yellow onion
¼ teaspoon salt
¼ teaspoon ground nutmeg
3 tablespoons butter, cut into 1/8-inch pieces
120 ml. milk
2 tablespoons flour
85 grams Swiss cheese slices, torn into small pieces
60 grams finely chopped green onion (optional)

Layer half the potatoes, 60 grams onion, 1/8 teaspoon salt, 1/8 teaspoon nutmeg, 1 tablespoon butter in a slow cooker. Repeat layers. Cover and cook on low setting for 7 hours or on high setting for 4 hours. Remove potatoes with slotted spoon to serving dish.   Blend milk and flour in small bowl until smooth. Stir mixture into slow cooker. Add cheese; stir to combine. If slow cooker is on setting, turn to high, cover and cook for about 10 minutes, until slightly thickened. Stir. Pour cheese mixture over potatoes and serve. Garnish with chopped green onions, if desired. Makes 5 to 6 servings.

VEGETABLE CROCKPOT

8 medium potatoes
450 grams chopped onion
4 carrots, sliced
2 ribs celery, sliced
4 chicken stock cubes
1 tablespoon parsley flakes
1 litre water
80 grams butter
450 grams ham, cubed
1 x can evaporated milk

Peel and cut potatoes into bite-sized pieces. Put all ingredients except evaporated milk in slow cooker. Cover and cook on low setting for 9 to 11 hours. Gently stir in evaporated milk during last hour. If desired, thicken during the last 20 minutes with a mixture of about 2 tablespoons of flour and 2 tablespoons cold water.

VEGETABLE CURRY

4 medium carrots, bias sliced into inch slices
2 medium potatoes, cut into ½ cubes
1 x 425 gram can garbanzo beans, drained
225 grams green beans, cut into 1 pieces
150 grams coarsely chopped onion
3 to 4 cloves garlic, crushed
2 tablespoons quick-cooking tapioca
2 teaspoons curry powder
1 teaspoon ground coriander
½ teaspoon crushed red pepper (optional)
¼ teaspoon salt
1/8 teaspoon ground cinnamon
400 grams can vegetable broth
450 grams can tomatoes, cut up
160 grams hot cooked rice

In a large crockpot combine carrots, garbanzo beans, potatoes, green beans, onion, garlic, tapioca, curry powder, coriander, red pepper (if desired), salt, and cinnamon. Pour broth over everything. Cover,

and cook on low-heat setting for 8 to 10 hours or on high-heat setting for 4 to 5 hours. Stir in undrained tomatoes. Cover, and allow to stand for 5 minutes. Serve with cooked rice. Makes 4 servings.

VEGETABLES PAPRIKOSH

4 to 5 large carrots, cut in ½ -inch pieces
6 to 8 large potatoes, cut in 1 inch cubes
5 large celery ribs, sliced
2 large onions, thinly sliced
1 to 3 tablespoons Hungarian paprika, or to taste
salt and pepper, to taste
2 cups water

Combine all ingredients in the slow cooker; add water and cook on high setting for 4 hours.

VEGETABLE SLOW COOKER

8 potatoes
1 onion, chopped
4 carrots, peeled and sliced
2 stalks celery, sliced
4 chicken stock cubes
1 tablespoon parsley flakes
5 cups water
90 grams butter or margarine
Ham, cubed to taste
1 x 368 gram can evaporated milk

Peel and cut potatoes into bite-sized pieces. Put all ingredients except evaporated milk into crockpot. Cover and cook on low setting for 10 to 12 hours. Stir in evaporated milk during last hour. Add flour to thicken, if desired.

VEGETABLE PASTA FOR CROCKPOT

2 tablespoons butter or margarine
1 zucchini, cut into ¼ inch slices
1 yellow squash, cut into ¼ inch slices
2 carrots, thinly sliced
115 grams fresh mushrooms, sliced
1 packet frozen broccoli
4 green onions, sliced
2 to 3 cloves garlic, crushed
½ teaspoon basil, dried
¼ teaspoon salt
½ teaspoon pepper
125 grams parmesan cheese, grated
340 grams feta cheese
125 grams mozzarella cheese, grated
250 ml. cream
2 egg yolks

Rub crock wall with butter. Put zucchini, yellow squash, carrots, mushrooms, broccoli, onions, garlic, seasonings and parmesan in the Crockpot. Cover, and cook on high setting for 2 hours. Cook fettuccine according to packet directions; drain. Add cooked fettuccine, mozzarella, cream and egg yolks. Stir to blend well. Allow to heat for 15 to 30 minutes. For serving turn to low setting for up to 30 minutes. Serves 6.

VEGETABLES, ITALIAN STYLE

1 teaspoon salt
1 medium eggplant, cut in 1 inch cubes
2 to 3 medium zucchini, halved and sliced ½ inch
1 large onion, sliced thinly
340 grams fresh mushrooms, sliced

1 tablespoon olive oil
4 plum tomatoes, sliced ¼ inch thick
170 grams mozzarella cheese, grated
500 ml. tomato sauce
1 teaspoon oregano
salt and pepper to taste

Toss eggplant and zucchini with the teaspoon of salt. Place in a large colander over a bowl to drain for about an hour. Drain and squeeze excess moisture out. In a large frying pan over medium heat, sauté onion, eggplant, zucchini, and mushrooms until slightly tender. In the slow cooker, layer 1/3 of the vegetables (including sliced tomatoes), 1/3 of the tomato sauce. and 1/3 of the cheese. Sprinkle with oregano, salt and pepper. Repeat layering 2 more times. Cover and cook on low setting for 6 to 8 hours. Serve over rice or pasta. Serves 6.

VEGETARIAN TACO SOUP

1 can black beans
1 can pinto beans
1 can navy beans
1 can black-eyed peas
1 can green beans
1 can corn
1 small onion, chopped
1 can tomato sauce
2 cups water
2 packets taco seasoning mix

Suggested condiments of your choice:
sour cream
grated cheese
Tabasco sauce
sliced jalapenos
green onions
crushed tortilla chips or corn chips

Drain and rinse first six ingredients in a large colander. Put in a crockpott. Add all other ingredients, stirring to mix well. Cook on high setting for 2 hours. Serves 8

WILD RICE CASSEROLE

150 grams uncooked long-grained rice
115 grams uncooked wild rice
1 envelope dry onion soup mix
1 tablespoon snipped parsley (optional)
1 litre water
1 bunch green onions, chopped
225 grams fresh or canned mushrooms, sliced
60 grams butter or margarine, melted

Combine all ingredients. Pour into lightly greased slow cooker. Cover and cook on high setting for 2½ hours, stirring occasionally.

ZUCCHINI CASSEROLE

1 red onion, sliced
1 green pepper, cut in thin strips
4 medium zucchinis, sliced and unpeeled
1 x 450 gram can diced tomatoes (do not drain)
1 teaspoon salt
½ teaspoon pepper
½ teaspoon basil
1 tablespoon. butter
60 grams grated Parmesan cheese

Combine all ingredients, except butter and cheese, in a slow cooker. Cook for 3 hours on low setting. Dot casserole with butter and sprinkle with cheese. Cook for a further 1½ hours on low setting. Makes 6 servings.

DESSERTS

APPLE BROWN BETTY

1.4 kilos cooking apples
10 slices of bread, cubed
½ teaspoon cinnamon
¼ teaspoon nutmeg
1/8 teaspoon salt
135 grams brown sugar
120 grams butter or margarine, melted

Wash apples, peel, core, cut into eighths; place in the bottom of the crockpot. Combine bread cubes, cinnamon, nutmeg, salt, sugar, butter; toss together. Place on top of apples in crock. Cover, and place crockpot into outer shell. Cook on low setting 2 to 4 hours. Makes 6 to 8 servings.

APPLE CAKE DESSERT

6 apples peeled, cored and sliced
sugar
cinnamon
225 grams of yellow cake mix
60 grams melted butter or margarine

Put slices of apples in crockpot. Pour half a packet of dry cake mix over apples. Drizzle butter over cake mix. Sprinkle cinnamon and sugar mixture over everything and cook on low 1 1/2 to 2 hours. Keep checking and it's done when the apples are soft.

APPLE DESSERT

6 apples, peeled and sliced
170 grams raw oatmeal
170 grams sugar
30 grams flour
1 teaspoon cinnamon
¼ teaspoon nutmeg
¼ teaspoon ginger
80 grams butter or margarine, melted

Mix oatmeal, sugar, flour, and spices in small bowl. Stir melted butter into mixture until it is crumbly. Put about half of sliced apples in crockpot and spoon about half of oatmeal mixture on top. Cover with the rest of the apples and top with the rest of the crumbly mixture. Cook on high setting for about 2½ hours.

APPLE CARAMEL DESSERT

2 medium apple
125 ml. apple juice
200 grams caramels
1 teaspoon vanilla
1/8 teaspoon ground cardamom
½ teaspoon ground cinnamon
80 grams creamy peanut butter
7 slices angel food cake
900 ml. vanilla ice cream

Peel, core and cut each apple into 18 wedges and set aside. Combine apple juice, unwrapped caramels, vanilla, cardamom and cinnamon. Drop peanut butter, 1 teaspoon at a time, over ingredients in crockpot and stir. Add apple wedges; cover and cook on setting for 5 hours. Stir thoroughly, then cook for one more hour. Serve approximately 85 grams of warm mixture over a slice of angel food cake or ice cream.

APPLE COCONUT CRISPS

4 large Granny Smith apples, peeled
& coarsely sliced
75 grams sweetened flaked coconut
1 tablespoon flour
85 grams brown sugar
125 ml. butterscotch or caramel ice
cream topping
½ teaspoon cinnamon
30 grams flour
120 grams quick rolled oats
2 tablespoons butter or margarine

In a casserole dish that fits in the crockpot, combine apples with coconut, 1 tablespoon flour, 90 grams brown sugar, and cinnamon. Drizzle with the ice cream topping. Combine remaining ingredients in a small bowl with a fork and sprinkle over apple mixture. Cover and cook on high setting for 2½ to 3 hours, until apples are tender. Serve warm with vanilla ice cream or whipped topping.

APPLE PIE

8 tart apples, peeled and sliced
1¼ teaspoons ground cinnamon
¼ teaspoon mixed spice
¼ teaspoon nutmeg
180 ml. milk
2 tablespoons butter, softened
150 grams sugar
2 eggs
1 teaspoon vanilla
115 grams Bisquick
225 grams Bisquick
80 grams brown sugar
3 tablespoons cold butter

Toss apples in large bowl with cinnamon, mixed spice, and nutmeg. Place in lightly greased crockpot. Combine milk, softened butter, sugar, eggs, vanilla, and the 115 grams of Bisquick. Spoon over apples. Combine the 225 grams of Bisquick and brown sugar. Cut the cold butter into mixture until crumbly. Sprinkle this mixture over top of apple mixture. Cover and cook on low setting for 6 to 7 hours or until apples are soft.

APPLE SAUCE

About 1.36 kg. apples, peeled, cored, and
sliced
90 grams sugar
1 cinnamon stick
2 tablespoons lemon juice
nutmeg

Put apples in cooker, sprinkle with sugar and add cinnamon stick. Sprinkle lemon juice on. Cover and cook on low setting for 6½ to 8 hours until apples form a thick sauce. Sprinkle with nutmeg to taste.

APPLE CARAMEL CROCK POT DESSERT

5 apples
250 ml. apple juice
400 grams caramel sweets
2 teaspoons vanilla
1 teaspoon cinnamon
2/3 cups peanut butter

Peel, core and cut each apple into 16 wedges. Set aside. Combine apple juice, caramels, vanilla and cinnamon in the crockpot. Add the apples. Add the peanut butter by teaspoons to the apples. Stir. Cover, and cook for 5 hours on low setting. Stir to mix thoroughly and cook for one more hour. Serve over angel food cake with vanilla ice cream.

APPLE-COCONUT CRISP

4 large Granny Smith apples, peeled & coarsely-sliced
75 grams sweetened flaked coconut
1 tablespoon flour
90 grams brown sugar
120 ml. butterscotch or caramel ice cream topping
½ teaspoon cinnamon
30 grams flour
75 grams quick rolled oats
2 tablespoons butter or margarine

In a 1 ½ quart baking dish or casserole that fits in your slow cooker, combine apples with coconut, 1 tablespoon flour, 90 grams brown sugar, and cinnamon. Drizzle with the ice cream topping. Combine remaining ingredients in a small bowl with a fork or pastry cutter and sprinkle over apple mixture. Cover and cook on high setting for 2 ½ to 3 hours, until apples are tender. Serve warm with vanilla ice cream or whipped topping.

APPLE CRANBERRY CRISP

3 apples
150 grams cranberries
135 grams brown sugar
90 grams rolled oats (quick cooking)
¼ teaspoon salt
1 teaspoon cinnamon
180 grams butter, softened

Peel, core and slice apples. Place apple slices and cranberries in crockpot. Mix remaining ingredients in separate bowl and sprinkle over top of apple and cranberries. Place 4 or 5 paper towels over the top of the crockpot, place an object (for example, a wooden spoon) across the top of the crockpot and set lid on top. This allows the steam to escape. Turn crockpot onto high setting and cook for about 2 hours. Serves 4.

APPLE CRANBERRY COMPOTE

6 cooking apples, peeled, sliced
150 grams fresh cranberries
200 grams sugar
½ teaspoon grated orange peel
120 ml. water
60 ml. port wine
sour cream to taste

Arrange apple slices and cranberries in slow cooker. Sprinkle sugar over fruit. Add orange peel, water and wine. Stir to mix ingredients. Cover and cook on low setting for 4 to 6 hours, until apples are tender. Serve warm fruits with the juices, topped with a dab of sour cream. Serves 6.

APPLE CRISP

6 apples, peeled and sliced
6 tablespoons butter
100 grams quick-cooking oats
1 tablespoon cinnamon
150 grams brown sugar
70 grams flour

Spray crockpot with non-stick cooking spray. Place prepared apples in the bottom of the crock pot. Melt butter in small mixing bowl. Stir in remaining ingredients until crumbly. Sprinkle evenly over fruit and press down lightly. Cook on high setting for about 3 hours. Serves 4 to 6.

APPLE DATE PUDDING

4 to 5 apples, peeled, cored and diced
135 grams sugar, to taste
75 grams chopped dates
75 grams toasted, chopped pecans
2 tablespoons flour
1 teaspoon baking powder
1/8 teaspoon salt
1/4 teaspoon nutmeg
2 tablespoon. melted butter
1 egg, beaten

In the slow cooker, place apples, sugar, dates and pecans; stir. In a separate bowl, mix together flour, baking powder, salt and nutmeg and stir into apple mixture. Drizzle melted butter over batter and stir. Stir in egg. Set cooker on low and cook for 3 to 4 hours. Serve warm. NOTE: If crispier nuts are desired, add toasted pecans at the end of the cooking period.

APPLE OATMEAL

500 ml. milk
2 tablespoons honey
1 tablespoon butter
¼ teaspoon salt
½ teaspoon cinnamon
60 grams dry old fashioned oats
80 grams chopped apples
115 grams chopped walnuts
2 tablespoons brown sugar
115 grams raisins (optional)

Spray crockpot with oil. Add all of the ingredients, stir, and cover. Cook on low setting for 5 to 6 hours. Serves 5.

APPLE-NUT CHEESECAKE

Crust:
120 grams graham cracker crumbs
½ teaspoon cinnamon
2 tablespoons sugar
3 tablespoons butter, melted
40 grams finely chopped pecans or walnuts

Filling:
450 grams cream cheese
30 grams brown sugar
100 grams granulated white sugar
2 large eggs
3 tablespoons double cream
1 tablespoon cornflour
1 teaspoon vanilla

Topping:
1 large apple, thinly sliced
1 teaspoon cinnamon
50 grams sugar
1 tablespoon finely chopped pecans or walnuts

Combine crust ingredients; pat into a 7-inch cake tin. Beat sugars into cream cheese until smooth and creamy. Beat in eggs, double cream, cornflour, and vanilla. Beat with a hand-held electric mixer for about 3 minutes on medium speed. Pour mixture into the prepared crust. Combine apple slices with sugar, cinnamon and nuts; place topping evenly over the top of cheesecake. Place the cheesecake on a rack (or "ring" of aluminium foil to keep it off the bottom of the pot) in the Crockpot. Cover and cook on high setting for 2 ½ to 3 hours. Allow to stand in the covered pot (after turning it off) for about 1 to 2 hours, until cool enough to handle. Cool thoroughly before removing pan sides. Chill before serving; store leftovers in the refrigerator.

APPLE PIE COFFEE CAKE

Apple Mixture:
1 can apple pie filling, apple slices broken up somewhat
½ teaspoon cinnamon
3 tablespoons brown sugar

Cake Batter:
2 small yellow cake mixes
2 eggs, beaten
120 ml. sour cream
3 tablespoons softened butter or margarine
120 ml. evaporated milk
1/2 teaspoon cinnamon
1 teaspoon butter or margarine for greasing slow cooker

Combine ingredients for apple mixture in a small bowl. Combine batter ingredients; mix well. Generously butter the sides and bottom of a large slow cooker. Spread about half the apple mixture in the bottom of the crockpot. Spoon half the batter over the apple mixture. Spoon the remaining apple mixture over the batter, then cover with remaining batter. Cover and cook on high for 2 to 2½ hours. Turn heat off, leave cover ajar slightly, and cool for about 15 minutes. Invert on a plate, retrieving any apples left in the bottom of the pot and placing on top of the cake. Makes a cake about 7 inches in diameter and 3½ inches high.

APPLE PUDDING CAKE

400 grams sugar
240 ml. vegetable oil
2 eggs
2 teaspoons vanilla
240 grams flour
1 teaspoon baking soda
1 teaspoon nutmeg
300 grams unpeeled apple, finely chopped
150 grams chopped nuts walnuts or pecans

Beat sugar, oil, eggs, and vanilla. Add apple with dry ingredients and mix well. Spray a two pound cake tin with cooking spray or grease and flour it well. Pour batter into tin, filling no more than 2/3 full. Place can in crockpot. Do not add water. Cover but leave cover ajar so steam can escape. Cook on high for 3½ to 4 hours. Don't peek before the last hour of baking. Cake is done when top is set. Let stand in can a few minutes before tipping pudding out on a plate. Serve half-rounds plain, with whipped topping, or a pudding sauce.

APRICOT NUT BREAD

165 grams dried apricots
120 grams flour
2 teaspoons baking powder
¼ teaspoon baking soda
½ teaspoon salt
100 grams sugar
180 ml. milk
1 egg, slightly beaten
1 tablespoon rated orange peel
1 tablespoon vegetable oil
55 grams whole wheat flour
150 grams coarsely chopped walnuts

Place the apricots on a chopping block. Sprinkle 1 tablespoon of flour over them. Dip a knife into the flour and chop the apricots finely. Flour the knife often to keep the cut up fruit from sticking together. Sift the remaining flour, baking powder, baking soda, salt and sugar into a large bowl. Combine the milk, egg, orange peel, and oil. Stir the flour mixture and the whole wheat flour. Fold in the cut up apricots, any flour left on the cutting block and the walnuts. Pour into a well greased, floured loaf tin. Cover and place on a rack in the slow cooker, but prop the lid open a fraction with a toothpick or a twist of foil to let excess steam escape. Cook on high setting for 4 to 6 hours. Cool on a rack for 10 minutes. Serve warm or cold. Makes 4 to 6 servings. Do not lift the lid while baking this bread.

119

BAKED APPLES (1)

2 tablespoon raisins
60 grams sugar
6 to 8 apples, washed and cored
1 teaspoon cinnamon
2 tablespoon butter

Mix raisins and sugar, and fill centre of apples.
Sprinkle with cinnamon and dot with butter.
Put in crockpot; add 120 ml. water. Cover, and
cook on low setting for 7 to 9 hours.

BAKED APPLES (2)

6 large cooking apples
190 ml. orange juice
2 teaspoon grated orange rind
1 teaspoon lemon rind grated
190 ml. rose wine
¼ teaspoon cinnamon
100 grams. brown sugar
whipped cream

Remove core from apples and place in slow
cooker. Mix together all other ingredients
except whipped cream. Pour over apples. Cover
crockpot and cook on low setting for about 3½
hours or until apples are tender. Cool and serve
with whipped cream.

BARLEY PUDDING

500 grams barley
2 litres milk
375 grams raisins
1 tablespoon cinnamon
1 teaspoon nutmeg

Cook barley, milk and raisins in slow cooker
until done. Stir in the rest of the ingredients.
Serve hot or cold for dessert or breakfast.

BAKED CUSTARD

500 ml. milk, scalded
3 eggs, slightly beaten
90 grams sugar
1 teaspoon vanilla
1/8 teaspoon salt
nutmeg or coconut

Scald milk and cool slightly. Combine eggs,
sugar, vanilla, and salt. Slowly stir in slightly
cooled milk. Pour into a buttered baking dish.
Sprinkle with nutmeg or coconut. Cover with
foil. Set baking dish on a trivet or meat rack in
crockpot. Pour hot water around baking dish, 1
inch deep. Cover crockpot and cook on high for
2 to 2½ hours or until knife inserted in custard
comes out clean. Serve warm or chilled. Makes
5 to 6 servings.

BANANA BREAD

210 grams flour
2 teaspoon baking powder
¼ teaspoon baking soda
½ teaspoon salt
80 grams shortening
160 grams sugar
2 eggs, well beaten
5 over-ripe bananas, well mashed
20 grams walnuts, coarsely chopped

Sift together flour, baking powder, baking soda
and salt. With an electric whisk on low, fluff
shortening in a small bowl, until soft and
creamy. Add sugar gradually. Beat in eggs in a
slow stream. With a fork, beat in 1/3 of the
flour mixture, ½ the bananas, another 1/3 of the
flour mixture, the rest of the bananas, then the
last of the flour mixture. Fold in walnuts. Turn
into a greased and floured 2½ quart mould and
cover. Place on a rack in crockpot. Cover
crockpot, but prop the lid open with a toothpick
or a twist of foil to let the excess steam escape.
Cook on high setting for 4 to 6 hours. Cool on a
rack for 10 minutes. Serve warm.

BANANA NUT BREAD

15 grams shortening
100 grams sugar
2 eggs
210 grams flour
1 teaspoon baking powder
½ teaspoon baking soda
½ teaspoon salt
4 mashed ripe bananas
20 grams chopped walnuts

Cream together shortening and sugar; add eggs and beat well. Sift dry ingredients; add to creamed mixture alternately with banana, blending well after each addition. Stir in nuts. Pour into well-greased 4 to 6 cup mould. Cover with foil and tie a string tightly around it to keep foil down. Pour 500 ml. hot water in crockpot. Place mould on rack or trivet in crockpot. Cover with crockpot lid and cook on high setting for 2 to 3 hours or until bread is done. Be sure not to check bread during the first 2 hours of cooking.

BLACKBERRY COBBLER

400 grams frozen blackberries, thawed and drained
110 grams sugar
85 ml. water
1 tsp. lemon juice
240 grams Bisquick Original baking mix
2 tablespoon sugar
85 ml. milk
ground cinnamon
whipping cream or vanilla ice cream, if desired

Mix blackberries, 110 grams sugar, the water, and lemon juice in crockpot. Cover and cook on low setting for 3 to 4 hours, or until mixture is boiling. Mix Bisquick and 2 tablespoons sugar in small bowl. Stir in milk just until dry ingredients are moistened. Drop dough by 6 spoonfuls onto hot berry mixture. Sprinkle with cinnamon. Cover and cook on high setting for 20 to 25

minutes. To serve, spoon dumpling into dessert dish. Spoon berry mixture over dumpling. Top with whipping cream or ice cream.

BLUEBERRY PUDDING

1 can blueberry pie filling
1 packet yellow cake mix
115 grams butter
115 grams chopped walnuts

Place pie filling in the slow cooker. Combine dry cake mix and butter, sprinkle over filling. Sprinkle the walnuts on top of that. Cover and cook on low setting for 2 to 3 hours. Serve warm in bowls. Top with whipped cream or vanilla ice cream.

BREAD PUDDING IN CARAMEL SAUCE

300 grams packed brown sugar
60 grams butter, softened
3 eggs
1 teaspoon vanilla or 3 tablespoons dark rum or whisky
1 teaspoon ground cinnamon
½ teaspoon freshly grated nutmeg
2 ½ cups milk
6 slices white bread, cut into 1-inch squares

In a bowl, beat sugar and butter until smooth and creamy. Add eggs, one at a time, and beat until incorporated. Add vanilla, cinnamon and nutmeg and beat until blended. Stir in milk. Place the bread in your slow cooker. Add milk mixture and stir to combine. Cover and cook on high setting for 4 hours. Serves 6.

BREAKFAST COBBLER

4 medium-sized apples, peeled and sliced
60 ml. honey
1 teaspoon cinnamon
2 tablespoons melted butter
160 grams toasted muesli cereal

Place apples in slow cooker and mix in remaining ingredients. Cover and cook on low setting for 7 to 9 hours 7-9 hours (overnight) or on high setting for 2 to 3 hours. Serve with milk. Makes 4 servings

CANDIED BANANAS

6 green-tipped bananas, peeled
75 grams flaked coconut
½ teaspoon cinnamon
¼ teaspoon salt
120 ml. dark corn syrup
60 grams flour or margarine, melted
2 teaspoons grated lemon peel
60 ml. lemon juice

Put bananas and coconut into large enough crockpot to fit in a single layer. Sprinkle with cinnamon and salt. Mix corn syrup, butter, lemon peel, and lemon juice; pour over bananas. Cover and cook on low setting for 1 to 2 hours.

CARAMEL APPLE EUPHORIA DESSERT

2 medium cooking apples
125 ml. apple juice
200 grams caramel candy squares
1 teaspoon vanilla extract
1/8 teaspoon ground cardamom
1/2 teaspoon ground cinnamon
85 ml. smooth peanut butter
7 slices angel-food cake or
950 ml. vanilla ice cream

Peel, core, and cut each apple into 18 wedges, and set aside. Combine apple juice, unwrapped caramels, vanilla, cardamom and cinnamon. Drop peanut butter 1 teaspoon at a time, over ingredients in crockpot. Stir. Add apple wedges; cover and cook on low setting for 5 hours. Stir thoroughly, then cover and cook on low setting for another hour. Serve approximately 90 grams of warm mixture over a slice of angel food cake or ice cream. Serves 7.

CARAMEL APPLES (TOFFEE APPLES)

800 grams cream caramels
60 ml. water
8 medium apples

In slow cooker, combine caramels and water. Cover and cook on high setting for 1 to 1 ½ hours, stirring frequently. Wash and dry apples. Insert stick into stem end of each apple. Turn control on low. Dip apple into hot caramel and turn to coat entire surface. Holding apple above pot, scrape off excess accumulation of caramel from bottom apple. Place on greaseproof paper to cool.

CARAMEL PIE

2 cans sweetened condensed milk
1 x 9 inch graham cracker crust
Dream Topping
1 (1.4 oz) English toffee bar, coarsely chopped

Pour condensed milk in a slow cooker. Cover and cook on low setting for 6 to 7 hours or until mixture is the colour of peanut butter, stirring mixture with a wire whisk every 30 minutes. Pour into graham cracker crust, cool. Spread whipped toping over top, and sprinkle with chopped toffee bar. Cover and chill. Makes 1 pie.

CARAMEL CUSTARD

4 medium eggs
1 teaspoon vanilla
375 ml. milk
900 grams granulated sugar
125 ml. boiling water

Beat the eggs with an electric whisk until thick. Add the vanilla and whisk until lemon coloured. Add the milk and 2 ½ cups of the sugar with the whisk on low, combine well. Butter a 2-quart mould. In a heavy medium-sized frying pan melt the remaining 2 cups of sugar over a very low heat. When it begins to bubble and turn brown, stir to combine all the sugar in the frying pan. When the caramelising sugar is a medium brown, pour half the caramel into the bottom of the mould. Into the other half of the caramelised sugar in the frying pan, pour ½ a cup of boiling water. Stir over low heat until the mixture bubbles. Allow it to cool, then chill for use as sauce. Pour the egg and milk mixture into the mould. Pour 2 cups of hot water into the slow cooker and place the mould on a trivet or rack in the bottom. Cover the pot, but prop the lid open a fraction with a toothpick or a twist of foil to allow excess steam to escape. Cook on high for 2 to 4 hours or until a silver knife inserted in the centre of the custard comes out clean. Chill, covered, in the refrigerator, then un-mould and serve with caramel sauce over the top. Makes 6 to 8 servings.

CARAMEL RUM FONDUE

200 grams cream caramels
100 grams miniature marshmallows
100 ml. double cream
2 teaspoons rum or ¼ teaspoon rum essence

Combine caramels and cream in crockpot. Cover and heat for 30 to 60 minutes, or until melted. Stir in marshmallows and rum. Cover and continue cooking for a further 30 minutes. Serve with apple wedges or pound cake.

CINNAMON APPLE BREAD PUDDING

2 tablespoons butter
2 apples, cored peeled, and chopped
150 grams brown sugar, divided
1½ teaspoons cinnamon, divided
2 large eggs
1 x can evaporated milk
¾ cup apple juice
2½ cups French bread, torn into ½ to 1 inch pieces

Melt butter in bottom of a casserole or soufflé dish which will fit in the slow cooker. Sprinkle with 2 tablespoons brown sugar and ½ teaspoon cinnamon. Add apples. Whisk eggs, milk, and apple juice together; mix in remainder of brown sugar, 1 teaspoon cinnamon, and the bread pieces. Place a trivet or aluminium foil ring in the slow cooker. Pour ¾ cup hot water into the slow cooker. Place the casserole dish on the ring in the slow cooker. Cover and cook on high for 2½ hours, until knife inserted comes out clean. Serve warm with vanilla ice cream or sweetened whipped cream.

CARROT PUDDING

4 large carrots, cooked and grated
1 small onion, grated
½ teaspoon salt
1/4tteaspoon nutmeg
1 tablespoon sugar
250 ml. milk
3 eggs, beaten

Mix together carrots, onion, salt, nutmeg, sugar, milk, and eggs. Pour into slow cooker and cook on high setting for 3 to 4 hours.

CHERRY CHOCOLATE DESSERT

1 can cherry pie filling
1 packet chocolate cake mix
125 ml. melted butter

Place pie filling in slow cooker. Combine dry cake mix and butter. Sprinkle over filling. Cover and cook on low setting for 3 hours.

CHERRY COBBLER

1 can cherry pie filling
1 carton cake mix for 1 layer cake, or sweet muffin mix
1 egg
3 tablespoons evaporated milk
½ teaspoon cinnamon
75 grams chopped nuts (optional)

Put pie filling in a large, lightly buttered crockpot and cook on high setting for 30 minutes. Mix together the remaining ingredients and spoon onto the hot pie filling. Cover and cook for 2 to 3 hours on low setting. You may also use a lightly greased soufflé dish in a larger crockpot. Serves 6.

CHERRY CHOCOLATE DESSERT

1 can cherry pie filling
1 packet chocolate cake mix
125 ml. Melted butter

Place pie filling in slow cooker. Combine dry cake mix and butter. Sprinkle over filling. Cover and cook on low setting for 3 hours.

CHOCOLATE-AMARETTO CHEESECAKE

Crust:
170 grams wafer-cookie crumbs
1/8 teaspoon almond essence
1 tablespoon sugar
3 tablespoons butter, melted

Filling:
125 grams ricotta cheese (light)
340 grams cream cheese
200 grams sugar
2 eggs
3 tablespoons double cream
60 ml. amaretto
60 grams plus 1 tablespoon cocoa
30 grams all-purpose flour
1 teaspoon vanilla
85 grams chocolate buttons (or similar)

Combine crust ingredients and pat into a 7-inch cake tin. Whisk the cheeses with the sugar until smooth; add eggs and cream and whisk for about 3 minutes on medium speed of an electric hand-held mixer. Add amaretto, cocoa, flour and vanilla, and whisk for about another minute. Stir in chocolate buttons, and pour into prepared pan. Place the cheesecake on a rack in the crockpot (or use a "ring" of aluminium foil to keep it off the bottom of the pot). Cover and cook on high for 2 ½ to 3 hours. Allow to stand in the covered pot (after turning it off) for about 1 to 2 hours, until cool enough to handle. Cool thoroughly before removing pan sides. Chill before serving; store leftovers in the fridge.

CHERRY CRISP

1 can cherry pie filling
130 grams brown sugar
75 grams quick-cooking oats
50 grams flour
1 teaspoon brown sugar
80 grams butter, softened

Lightly butter a 3 large slow cooker. Place cherry pie filling in the slow cooker. Combine dry ingredients and mix well; cut in butter with a pastry cutter or fork. Sprinkle crumbs over the cherry pie filling. Cook for 5 hours on low setting.

CHOCOLATE APPLE CAKE

6 tablespoons butter
115 grams sugar
115 grams brown sugar
250 ml. unsweetened apple sauce
1 teaspoon cinnamon
1 teaspoon pure vanilla essence
3 eggs
30 grams unsweetened chocolate, melted
70 grams flour
2 teaspoons baking soda
1 teaspoon baking powder
pinch of salt
95 ml. buttermilk
190 ml. semisweet chocolate chips
115 grams chopped pecans
Icing sugar

In a large bowl, whisk together butter and sugars with an electric mixer on high speed for one to two minutes, or until fluffy. Beat in apple sauce, cinnamon, vanilla and eggs until well mixed. Whisk in melted chocolate until blended. Add flour, baking soda and baking powder, and the salt. With your whisk on low speed, whisk in the dry ingredients, adding buttermilk as you whisk.Whisk just until evenly mixed. By hand stir in chocolate chips and pecans. Scrape the batter into a large, well-buttered crockpot and smooth top. Cover and cook on the high setting for 2¼ to 2½ hours, or until a cake tester (toothpick) inserted in the centre comes out clean. (Do not cook on the low heat setting for a longer time) Remove lid and let cake stand in crockpot until just barely warm. To unmould: Run a sharp knife around the inside edges of the crockpot and with a large spatula, carefully lift out the cake in one piece. Sprinkle with icing sugar over top and cut into wedges to serve.

CHOCOLATE APPLE SAUCE CAKE

6 tablespoon butter
200 grams sugar
250 ml. unsweetened apple sauce
1 teaspoon cinnamon
1 teaspoon vanilla
3 eggs
30 grams unsweetened chocolate, melted
120 grams flour
2 teaspoons baking soda
1 teaspoon baking powder
pinch of salt
80 grams buttermilk
170 grams semisweet chocolate chips
75 grams chopped walnuts
icing sugar

In a large bowl, whisk together the butter and sugar with an electric mixer on high speed for 1 to 2 minutes, or until fluffy. Beat in the apple sauce, cinnamon, vanilla and eggs until well mixed. Whisk in the melted chocolate until blended. Add the flour, baking soda and powder, and salt. With the mixer on low speed, beat in the dry ingredients, adding the buttermilk as you beat. Beat just until evenly mixed. By hand, stir in chocolate chips and nuts. Scrape the batter into a large, well-buttered slow cooker and smooth the top. Cover and cook on high setting for 2¼ to 2½ hours, or until a cake tester inserted in the centre comes out clean. (Do not cook on the low heat setting for a longer time) Remove the lid and let the cake stand in the slow cooker until just barely warm. To un-mould, run a sharp knife around the inside edges of the crock and with a large spatula, carefully lift out the cake in one piece. Sprinkle with icing sugar over the top and cut into wedges to serve.

CHOCOLATE BROWNIE PUDDING CAKE

100 grams brown sugar
180 ml. water
2 tablespoon cocoa
680 grams brownie mix
1 egg
60 grams peanut butter
1 tablespoon soft margarine
60 ml. water
115 grams milk chocolate chips, if desired

Combine 180 ml. water, brown sugar, and cocoa in a saucepan. Bring to the boil. In the meantime combine the remaining ingredients in a small bowl. Whisk together or mix well with a spoon. Spread the batter evenly in the bottom of a lightly buttered slow cooker. Pour boiling mixture over the batter. Cover and cook on high about 2 hours; turn heat off and let stand for about 30 minutes. Spoon into dessert dishes while warm; serve with whipped cream or ice cream. Serves 6 to 8.

CHOCOLATE CLUSTERS

900 grams white almond bark
1 x 115 gram bar German chocolate
1 packet chocolate chips (340 grams)
700 grams dry roasted peanuts

Put all ingredients in crockpot; cover and cook on high setting for one hour. Do not stir. Turn crockpot to low setting and stir every 15 minutes for one hour. Drop on greaseproof paper and let cool. Store in a tightly covered container.

CHOCOLATE COVERED CHERRY COBBLER

1 can cherry pie filling (you could use two cans if you like)
1 packet chocolate cake mix
125 ml. melted butter

Spread pie filling in the bottom of your crockpot. Mix butter and chocolate cake mix together with a whisk – the mixture will be crumbly. Cook on low setting for 2-3 hours. Serves 6.

CHOCOLATE CHIP PEANUT BUTTER CAKE

120 grams butter
100 grams sugar
100 grams brown sugar
3 eggs, beaten
120 grams peanut butter
180 ml. light sour cream
1 teaspoon vanilla essence
680 grams all-purpose flour
1 teaspoon baking powder
1 teaspoon baking soda
½ teaspoon salt
225 grams chocolate chips

Cream butter and sugars. Beat eggs in well. Mix in peanut butter, sour cream and vanilla. Combine flour, baking powder, soda and salt together and add to creamed mixture. Stir in most of the chocolate chips, reserving a few for the top. Spoon mixture into a greased and floured 2 1/2 to 3-quart soufflé dish or mould (which will fit in your crockpot). Place a small trivet (or fashion a little "ring" from aluminium foil) in the Crockpot, place the dish on the trivet, then cover the dish with 4 layers of paper towels. Cover loosely to allow steam to escape and cook on high setting for about 4 hours. Test with a toothpick for doneness. Cool in pot until dish is cool enough to handle, then transfer to a wire rack to cool completely.

CHOCOLATE HEAVEN

1 packet chocolate cake mix
1 x 85 gram packet instant chocolate pudding mix
4 eggs
1 cup water
500 ml. sour cream
190 ml. cup vegetable oil
190 ml. cup semi-sweet chocolate chips
¼ cup milk chocolate chips
½ cup walnuts, chopped

Spray a large crockpot with non-stick cooking spray and set aside. In a large bowl, combine the cake mix and pudding mix. In a medium bowl, beat the eggs with the water, then add the sour cream and oil and whisk until smooth. Add to the dry ingredients and whisk well. Stir in the chocolate chips and walnuts. Pour into crockpot. Cover slow cooker and cook on low setting for 6 to 8 hours, until top springs back when touched very lightly with finger. Serves 8 to 10.

CHOCOLATE RASPBERRY STRATA

500 grams bread cubes
125 ml. double cream
125 ml. milk
340 grams chocolate chips
4 eggs
50 grams sugar
fresh raspberries (do not substitute frozen), rinsed and drained
1 teaspoon vanilla essence
whipped cream

Place half of the bread cubes in a well-buttered slow cooker. Sprinkle on half of the chocolate chips and raspberries. Cover with the remaining bread cubes, then top with the remaining chocolate chips and raspberries. In a medium bowl, whisk together the cream, milk, eggs, sugar, and vanilla until well blended. Pour evenly over the bread mixture in the cooker. Cover and cook on the high heat setting about 1 ¾ to 2 hours, or until set. (Do not cook on the low heat setting for a longer time.) Allow to stand 5 to 10 minutes before serving. Garnish with whipped cream to serve.

CHOCOLATE PEANUT BUTTER CAKE

500 grams chocolate cake mix
240 ml. water
85 grams creamy peanut butter
115 grams chopped nuts

Combine all ingredients in bowl, mixing well. Beat for about 2 minutes. Pour batter into greased and floured 1.5 kilo coffee tin. Place can in crockpot. Cover top of can with 8 paper towels. Cover crockpot and bake on high setting for 2 to 3 hours

.CHOCOLATE RICE PUDDING

800 grams cooked white rice
150 grams brown sugar
35 grams cocoa powder
3 tablespoons unsalted butter, melted
1 teaspoon vanilla essence
2 x cans evaporated milk
115 grams slivered almonds or your favourite nuts

Lightly spray the inside of a crockpot with cooking spray. Combine all ingredients in the crockpot, cover the crockpot and cook on low setting for 2½ to 3 hours, or until all the liquid has been absorbed. Stir before serving. Serve either warm or chilled. To chill, allow the rice pudding to cool for about 2 hours, then spoon it into a bowl, cover and refrigerate until ready to serve. Serve with cream and a sprinkling of slivered almonds or nuts of your choice. Serves 10.

CHRISTMAS BREAD PUDDING

9 slices wholemeal bread
8 slices white bread
3 egg yolks, beaten
350 ml. single cream
170 grams dark sultanas
85 grams whole candied red cherries, halved
180 ml. cream sherry
250 ml. water
2 egg yolks, beaten
60 grams icing sugar, sifted
2 tablespoons cream sherry
90 grams sugar
dash salt
1½ teaspoons vanilla essence
170 grams sultanas
¼ teaspoon vanilla
120 ml. double cream

Remove crusts from bread. Cover bread slices with paper towels and allow to stand overnight.

Custard: in a heavy medium saucepan combine three egg yolks, light cream, sugar and salt. Cook and stir over medium heat. Continue cooking until mixture coats a metal spoon. Remove from heat, and cool at once by setting saucepan in a sink of iced water and stirring for 1 to 2 minutes. Stir in 1½ teaspoons vanilla. Cover surface with clear plastic wrap. In small a bowl combine sultanas. Place cherries in another bowl. Heat 180 ml. sherry till warm. Pour 160 ml. sherry over cherries. Set aside. Cut bread into ½ inch cubes. In a bowl, fold bread into custard, until coated. Grease a 6½ cup tower mould (without tube). Drain raisins and cherries, reserving sherry. Arrange ¼ of cherries in bottom of the mould, sprinkle 85 grams raisins into the mould. Add ¼ of bread cube mixture. Sprinkle with 2 tablespoons reserved sherry. Repeat layers three times, arranging cherries and raisins near edges of the mould. Lightly press last layer with back of spoon. Pour remaining reserved sherry over everything. Cover mould tightly with foil, and set mould in cooker. Pour 120 ml. water around mould. Cover, and cook on low setting for 5½ hours or until pudding springs back when touched. Meanwhile make the sherry sauce: in a mixing bowl combine 2 egg yolks, icing sugar, 2 tablespoons sherry and ¼ teaspoon vanilla. In small bowl, beat cream until small peaks form. Gently fold cream into egg yolk mixture. Cover and chill until serving time. Remove mould from cooker, allow to stand for 10 minutes. Carefully unmould to serving platter. Serve warm with sherry sauce. Serves 12.

CHUNKY STYLE APPLE SAUCE

8 to 10 large cooking apples, peeled, cored, and sliced or cut in chunks
120 ml. water
1 teaspoon cinnamon
225 grams sugar

Put ingredients in crockpot. Cover and cook on low setting for 8 to 10 hours, or on high setting for 3 to 4 hours. Serve warm. Add cream if desired.

CINNAMON-APPLE BREAD PUDDING

2 tablespoons butter
2 apples, cored, peeled, and chopped
135 grams brown sugar, divided
1½ teaspoons cinnamon, divided
2 large eggs
340 grams can evaporated milk
180 ml. apple juice
680 grams French bread torn in ½ to 1- inch pieces

Melt butter in bottom of a casserole or soufflé dish which will fit in the slow cooker. Sprinkle with 2 tablespoons brown sugar and ½ teaspoon cinnamon. Add apples. Whisk eggs, milk, and apple juice together; mix in remainder of brown sugar, 1 teaspoon cinnamon, and the bread pieces. Place a trivet or aluminium foil ring in the slow cooker. Pour 180 ml. hot water into the slow cooker. Place the casserole dish on the ring in the slow cooker. Cover and cook on high for 2½ hours, until knife inserted comes out clean. Serve warm with vanilla ice cream or sweetened whipped cream.

CORN PUDDING

225 grams. cream cheese, softened
2 eggs, beaten
90 grams sugar
1 packet corn bread mix
450 grams can cream style corn
560 grams sweet corn
250 ml. milk
2 tablespoons margarine, melted
1 teaspoon salt
¼ teaspoon nutmeg

Lightly grease crockpot. In a bowl, blend cream cheese, eggs and sugar. Add remaining ingredients and mix well. Pour into crockpot. Cover and cook on high setting for 3 to 4 hours. Serves 10 to 12

COUNTRY APPLES

900 grams to 1.2 kg. apples
2 tablespoons flour
90 grams sugar
85 grams raisins
¼ teaspoon cinnamon
170 grams oatmeal
3 tablespoon butter
135 grams brown sugar

Peel, slice and coat apples with flour and 90 grams sugar. Stir in the raisins, cinnamon, and oatmeal. Pour 250 ml. water into the crockpot. Add apple mix. Pour melted butter over apples and then brown sugar. Cook on low setting for 4 to 6 hours. Serves 6. You can serve over vanilla ice cream, use as a crepe filling or over porridge for breakfast.

CRANAPPLE SAUCE

10 to 12 medium apples
160 grams cranberry juice
juice of half a lemon
2 tablespoons sugar, or up to 60 grams if you want it sweet
250 grams dried cranberries

Wash the apples and chop them up without peeling. Squeeze lemon juice over them as you cut them. Put apples in crockpot with cranberry juice (use 150 grams if you want the apple sauce thick, more if you want it thin). Stir in sugar to suit your taste. Stew the apples on low setting for 6 to 8 hours. About an hour or two before serving, stir in cranberries or raisins. The apple sauce is a very pretty pink and the cranberries and juice give it a nice zing. This recipe warms up nicely, or you can eat it cold.

COCONUT DESSERT

500 ml. milk
75 grams butter or margarine
2 teaspoons vanilla extract
4 egg
200 grams coconut; flaked
150 grams sugar
100 grams Bisquick baking mix

Place all ingredients in a blende, and mix well. Pour into slow cooker, and cook on low setting for 8 to 10 hours.

CREAMY ORANGE CHEESECAKE

Crust:
170 grams cookie or graham cracker crumbs
2 tablespoons sugar
3 tablespoons melted butter

Filling:
450 grams cream cheese (light)
170 grams sugar
2 eggs
1 egg yolk
60 ml. orange juice concentrate
1 teaspoon orange or lemon zest, or dried grated rind
1 tablespoon flour
½ teaspoon vanilla

Combine crumbs with sugar; mix in melted butter until well moistened. Pat into a 7- inch cake tin. In a medium bowl, cream together the cream cheese and sugar. Add eggs and yolk and beat for about 3 minutes on medium with a hand-held electric mixer. Beat in orange juice, zest, flour, and vanilla. Beat for another 2 minutes. Pour batter into prepared crust; place on a rack or aluminium foil ring in the slow cooker (so it doesn't rest on the bottom of the pot). Cover and cook on high setting for 2½ to 3 hours. Turn off and leave for 1 to 2 hours, until cool enough to remove. Cool completely and remove the sides of the pan. Chill before serving, and store leftovers in the refrigerator.

CRANBERRIES

1 packet fresh cranberries
500 grams sugar
60 ml. water

Combine cranberries with sugar and water in crockpot. Cover and cook on high setting for 2 to 3 hours until some pop. Serve with turkey or chicken.

CROCKPOT SCRABBLE

160 grams wheat breakfast cereal
160 grams corn breakfast cereal
160 grams rice breakfast cereal
600 grams thin pretzel sticks
375 grams salted peanuts or mixed nuts
1 teaspoon garlic salt
1 teaspoon celery salt
½ teaspoon seasoned salt
2 tablespoons grated parmesan cheese
200 ml. melted butter
80 ml. Worcestershire sauce

In a large (double) paper bag, mix together pretzels, cereals, and nuts along with the garlic salt, celery salt, seasoned salt, and grated cheese. Empty bag into a large mixing bowl and sprinkle the melted butter and Worcestershire sauce over all mixing gently with your hands. Empty bowl into slow cooker and cook on low setting for 3 or 4 hours. Tear open paper bags you used to originally mix the scrabble and spread them out onto a counter. Spread heated crockpot scrabble onto torn open bags and let dry for a minimum of one hour, letting the paper absorb any excess moisture. Store in airtight containers. Keeps for several weeks without going stale.

CURRIED FRUIT BAKE

450 grams pitted prunes
300 grams dried apricots
2 cans pineapple chunks, drained
1 large can sliced peaches
225 grams brown sugar
½ teaspoon curry powder
1 litre ginger ale

Combine all ingredients in slow cooker. Cover and cook on low setting for 4 to 5 hours or on auto for 3 hours.

CUSTARD

3 eggs, lightly beaten
90 grams sugar
1 teaspoon vanilla
500 ml. milk
¼ teaspoon ground nutmeg

In a mixing bowl combine eggs, sugar, vanilla and milk; mix well. Pour into a large, lightly buttered baking dish or soufflé which will fit in the crockpot, and sprinkle with the nutmeg. Place a rack or ring of aluminium foil in the crockpot, then add 350 ml. to 500 ml. of hot water to the pot. Cover the baking dish with aluminium foil and place on the rack in the slow cooker. Cover and cook on high setting for 2½ to 3 hours, or until set. Serves 4 to 6.

DECADENT CHOCOLATE DELIGHT

1 packet chocolate cake mix
250 ml. sour cream
500 ml. water
4 eggs
325 ml. vegetable oil
1 x 4-serving size packet chocolate flavour instant pudding mix
170 grams chocolate chips
ice cream, any flavour, softened (optional)

Lightly grease the inside of your slow cooker. Combine cake mix, sour cream, water, eggs and oil in a large bowl until well blended. Stir in pudding mix until well blended. Stir in chocolate chips. Pour mixture into slow cooker. Cover and cook on low setting for 6 to 8 hours or on high setting for 3 to 4 hours. Serve hot or warm with ice cream if desired. Makes 12 servings.

FRIED APPLES

1.5 kg. granny smith apples, peeled, cored, and sliced
1 teaspoon cinnamon
dash of fresh grated nutmeg (optional)
3 tablespoons cornflour
200 grams granulated sugar
1 to 2 tablespoons of butter, cut in small pieces

Use these apples as a topping, a filling, or alone topped with whipped cream. Place apple slices in the slow cooker, stir in remaining ingredients and dot with the butter. Cover and cook on low setting for about 6 hours, or until the apples are tender but not mushy. Stir about halfway through cooking.

FRESH APPLE COFFEE CAKE

120 grams biscuit mix
160 ml. apple sauce
85 ml. cup milk
2 tablespoons sugar
2 tablespoons softened butter or margarine
2 apples, peeled, cored and diced
1 teaspoon cinnamon
1 teaspoon vanilla
1 egg, lightly beaten

Strudel:
60 grams biscuit mix
60 grams brown sugar
2 tablespoons firm butter or margarine
1 teaspoon cinnamon
chopped nuts, if desired

Combine first 9 ingredients. Spread in a lightly greased slow cooker. Combine strudel ingredients with a fork or pastry blender, and sprinkle over the batter. Cover and cook on high setting for about 2½ hours, until a toothpick inserted in the centre comes out clean.

FRUITCAKE PUDDING

4 slices bread, torn up
½ teaspoon salt
250 ml. milk
2 teaspoons ground cinnamon
2 eggs, slightly beaten
1 teaspoon. ground cloves
200 grams light brown sugar
1 teaspoon ground mace
65 ml.. orange juice
250 grams raisins
170 grams suet, finely chopped
225 grams dates, pitted, cut up
60 grams mixed candied fruits
1 teaspoon vanilla essence
60 grams walnuts, coarsely chopped

120 grams flour
1 teaspoons baking soda

Soak bread in milk, and beat. Stir in eggs, sugar, juice, suet, and vanilla essence. In a large bowl, combine flour with baking soda, salt and spices. Add fruits and nuts. Mix well. Stir in bread mixture. Pour into well-greased that will fit into your slow cooker. Cover with foil, and tie with string. Place on a metal rack or trivet in the crockpot with 1 inch of water. Cover and cook on high setting for 5 to 6 hours. Cool in pan for 10 minutes, then remove from mould. Makes 10 to 12 servings.

GINGERY BREAD PUDDING WITH ORANGE

6 slices wholemeal bread or white bread
60 grams butter, softened
60 grams orange marmalade
60 grams finely chopped candied ginger
3 eggs
½ teaspoon vanilla or 2 tablespoons orange-flavored liqueur
100 grams packed brown sugar
625 ml. milk

Spread bread with butter and marmalade, then cut into 1-inch squares and place in slow cooker. Add candied ginger. In a bowl, beat eggs with vanilla and brown sugar. Blend in milk. Pour mixture over bread and toss to combine. Cover and cook on high setting for 4 hours, until pudding is set and edges are browning. Serve hot. Serves 6.

GINGER BROWN BREAD

1 packet gingerbread mix
60 grams yellow corn meal
1 teaspoon salt
375 ml. milk
75 grams raisins

Combine gingerbread mix with corn meal and salt in large bowl. Stir in milk until mixture is evenly moist. Beat at medium speed with electric mixer for 2 min. Stir in raisins. Pour into a greased and floured 7 cup mould. Cover with foil and tie. Put a trivet or metal rack in your crockpot. Pour 500 ml. hot water in the crockpot. Place the filled mould on the rack or the trivet. Cover the pot and cook on high setting for 3 to 4 hours or until the bread is done. Remove from pot and cool on a rack for 5 min. Loosen the edges with a knife and turn out on a rack and cool slightly. Serve warm with butter or cream cheese.

HEAVENLY PEACH CRISP

1 x can peaches, sliced and drained
110 grams brown sugar
50 grams flour
2 ½ teaspoons lemon juice
½   teaspoon cinnamon
2/3   cup granola cereal, divided

Spray slow cooker with nonstick cooking spray. Combine all ingredients, EXCEPT 1/3 cup granola in slow cooker. Sprinkle 1/3 cup granola on top. Cook on low setting for 4 to 6 hours. Serve with ice cream! Serves 2.

HOME-STYLE BREAD PUDDING

2 eggs, slightly beaten
2 60 ml. milk
1 teaspoon vanilla
½ teaspoon cinnamon
¼ teaspoon salt
160 grams 1-inch bread cubes
100 grams brown sugar
75 grams raisins or chopped dates

In a medium mixing bowl, combine eggs with milk, vanilla, cinnamon, salt, bread, sugar, and raisins or dates. Pour into 2 litre baking or soufflé dish. Place metal trivet (or aluminium foil shaped in a ring to keep the dish off the bottom of the pot) or rack in bottom of slow cooker. Add 120 ml. hot water. Set baking dish on trivet. Cover crockpot, and cook on high for about 2 hours. Serve pudding warm or cool. Makes 4 to 6 servings.

HOT FRUIT COMPOTE

1 can peaches, drained
1 can pears, drained
1 can pineapple chunks, drained
225 grams brown sugar
1 teaspoon cinnamon
115 grams margarine
1 can cherry pie filling

Cut all fruit into bite-size pieces. Add rest of ingredients. Stir all together. Cover and cook on low setting for 3 to 6 hours. Use as a side dish for breakfast or a meal, or as a topping for a dessert.

HOT FUDGE SUNDAE CAKE

140 grams plain flour
120 grams sugar
2 tablespoons cocoa
2 teaspoons baking powder
½ teaspoon salt
125 ml. milk
2 tablespoons vegetable oil
1 teaspoon vanilla
60 grams chopped nuts
150 grams packed brown sugar
35 grams baking cocoa
375 ml. hot water
cooking spray

Spray inside of a large crockpot with cooking spray. Mix flour, sugar, 2 tablespoons cocoa, baking powder and salt in medium bowl. Stir in milk, oil and vanilla until smooth. Stir in nuts. Spread batter evenly in slow cooker. Mix brown sugar and ¼ cup cocoa in small bowl. Stir in hot water until smooth. Pour evenly over batter in crock. Cover and cook on high setting for 2 to 2½ hours or until toothpick inserted in center comes out clean. Turn off crockpot. Allow cake to stand uncovered 30 to 40 minutes to cool slightly before serving. Spoon warm cake into dessert dishes. Spoon sauce over top. 6 servings.

INDIAN PUDDING

750 ml. milk
115 grams cornmeal
½ teaspoon salt
3 eggs
60 grams. light brown sugar
750 ml. molasses
2 tablespoon. butter
½ teaspoon cinnamon
¼ teaspoon mixed spice
½ teaspoon ginger

Lightly grease crockpot, and preheat on high setting for 20 minutes. Meanwhile bring milk, cornmeal and salt to the boil. Boil, stirring constantly, for 5 minutes. Cover and simmer an additional 10 minutes. In a large bowl, combine remaining ingredients. Gradually beat in hot cornmeal mixture and whisk until smooth. Pour into crockpot and cook on high setting for 2 to 3 hours or on low setting for 6 to 8 hours.

LUSCIOUS LEMON CHEESECAKE

Crust:
120 grams vanilla wafer crumbs
½ teaspoon lemon zest
1 tablespoons sugar
3 tablespoons butter, melted

Filling:
450 grams cream cheese
170 grams sugar
2 large eggs
1 tablespoon flour or cornflour
1 teaspoon fresh lemon zest
2 tablespoons fresh lemon juice

Combine crust ingredients. Pat into a 7-inch cake tin. Beat cream cheese and sugar together until smooth; beat in eggs and continue beating on medium speed of a hand-held electric mixer for about 3 minutes. Beat in remaining ingredients and continue beating for about 1 minute. Pour batter into the prepared crust. Place the cheesecake on a rack in the crockpot. Cover and cook on high setting for 2½ to 3 hours. Allow to stand in the covered pot after turning it off for a couple of hours, until cool enough to handle. Cool thoroughly before removing pan sides. Chill in the refrigerator before serving, and refrigerate any leftovers.

NEW YORK STYLE CHEESECAKE

2 large packets and 1 small packet cream cheese, softened
150 grams sugar
3 tablespoons flour
1 teaspoon freshly grated lemon peel
½ teaspoon freshly grated orange peel
3 eggs
crust

With electric mixer, beat softened cream cheese, sugar, flour and grated peels until smooth. Add eggs, one at a time, and beat until fluffy. Pour into baked crust in cake tin and cover. Place inside slow cooker. Cover and cook on high setting for 2½ to 3 hours. Remove pan and uncover. Allow to cool, then remove from mould on serving plate. Serve well chilled. If desired, top with strawberries. Serves 8 - 10.

OLD FASHIONED CROCKPOT APPLE BUTTER

14 cooking apples
620 grams sugar
250 ml. apple juice
1 tablespoon cinnamon
1 tablespoon cloves
1 teaspoon mixed spice

Wash and core apples, cut into quarters. Slightly grease crockpot, and put in apples and apple juice. Cook on high setting for 5 hours. Add other ingredients and cook for a further 6 hours on high setting. Stir each hour. Pack in ½ pint jars and seal. Makes 5 x ½ pint jars.

MINISTER'S DELIGHT

1 can cherry or apple pie filling
1 packet yellow cake mix
120 grams butter or margarine, melted
115 grams chopped walnuts (optional)

Place pie filling in a slow cooker. Combine dry cake mix and butter (mixture will be crumbly); sprinkle over filling. Sprinkle with walnuts if desired. Cover and cook on low for setting for 2 to 3 hrs. Serve in bowls.

PUDDING CAKE

120 grams flour
120 grams sugar
75 grams coarsely chopped pecans, or walnuts
60 grams unsweetened cocoa
2 teaspoons baking powder
½ teaspoon salt
120 ml. milk
60 ml. oil
1 teaspoon vanilla essence
250 ml. boiling water
120 ml. chocolate syrup
whipped cream or ice cream

Mix together first 6 ingredients in 6-cup mould. Stir in milk, oil and vanilla. Mix boiling water and chocolate syrup. Pour over batter. Place a small trivet in the bottom of the slow cooker, and add 500 ml. of warm water. Place mould in cooker and cover with 4 layers of paper towels. Cover cooker and cook on high setting for 3 to 4 hours. Serve warm with cream.

ORCHARD CRUMBLE

Fruit Mixture:
3 firm Bartlett pears, peeled, cored, and thickly sliced
2 large tart cooking apples, peeled, cored, and sliced
1½ cups fresh cranberries
½ teaspoon ground cinnamon
½ cup sugar
2 tablespoons cornflour

Topping:
1 cup all-purpose flour
½ cup quick-cooking rolled oats
1 cup firmly packed light brown sugar
½ teaspoon ground cinnamon
½ cup cold unsalted butter, cut into pieces

Coat slow cooker with butter-flavored cooking spray or grease with butter. Make the fruit mixture: put the fruit in the cooker; sprinkle with cinnamon, sugar, and cornflour; toss to coat the fruit. Cover and cook on high setting for 30 minutes. Make the topping: in a food processor, combine the flour, rolled oats, brown sugar, and cinnamon; add in butter and pulse to make coarse crumbs. After the 30 minutes, spread the topping evenly over the fruit, leaving a ½-inch border without topping to prevent burning. Cover, decrease heat to low setting, and cook for a further 2 ½ to 3 ½ hours until the fruit is tender. Test by sticking a knife into the center of the crumble, when it passes through the fruit with little resistance, the crumble is done. Uncover and let cool for 10 minutes before serving. Serve with ice cream or whipped cream if desired. Serves 6 – 8.

PEACH BUTTER

900 grams unsweetened peaches
600 grams white sugar
350 ml. apricot nectar
2 tablespoons orange or lemon juice
1 teaspoon vanilla

Put peaches through food processor. Mix all ingredients together well and put in crockpot.

Bring to the boil, uncover and continue to boil for 4 hours or until thick. Remove cover.

PEACH CRUMBLE

900 grams firm to ripe peaches, peeled, pitted, and thickly sliced

Topping:
150 grams quick-cooking rolled oats
150 grams flour
150 grams firmly packed light brown sugar
1 teaspoon baking powder
½ teaspoon ground cinnamon or apple pie spice
1 pinch ground nutmeg
¼ teaspoon salt
100 grams cold unsalted butter, cut into pieces
vanilla ice cream (or whipped cream)

Coat the slow cooker with cooking spray or grease with butter. Put the fruit in the slow cooker, cover, and cook on high setting for 30 minutes. Meanwhile, make the topping: in a bowl, combine the rolled oats, flour, brown sugar, baking powder, cinnamon, nutmeg, and salt. Cut in the butter using a pastry blender or your fingertips, and set aside. After the 30 minutes, spread the topping evenly over the fruit, leaving a ½-inch border without topping to prevent burning. Cover and decrease the heat setting to low, then cook for 2½ to 3 hours until the fruit is tender. Test by sticking a knife into the center of the crumble; when the knife passes through the fruit with little resistance, the crumble is done. Uncover and allow to cool for 10 minutes before serving. If desired, top with ice cream or whipped cream. Serves 6 to 8.

PUMPKIN TEA BREAD

115 ml. oil
115 grams sugar
115 grams brown sugar
2 beaten eggs
225 grams canned pumpkin
150 grams sifted flour
1/2 teaspoon salt
1/2 teaspoon cinnamon
1/2 teaspoon nutmeg
1 teaspoon soda
225 grams chopped walnuts

Blend oil and two sugars. Stir in beaten eggs and pumpkin. Sift dry ingredients together. Add and then stir in nuts. Pour batter into greased and floured 285 grams. coffee can. Place can in crockpot. Cover top of can with 6 to 8 paper towels; place lid on top. Bake on high setting for 2½ - 3½ hours. No peeking until last hour!

greased and floured ½ -pint straight-sided canning jars. Cover jars tightly with greased foil. Place a piece of crumpled foil in a large crockpot with liner in place. Place jars on top of crumpled foil. Coverand cook on high setting for 1½ to 1¾ hours or until a wooden toothpick inserted near centers comes out clean. Remove jars from cooker; cool 10 minutes in jars. Remove bread from jars. Cool thoroughly on wire rack. Makes 2 loaves.

PUMPKIN BREAD

120 grams flour
1½ teaspoon baking powder
1 teaspoon pumpkin pie spice
100 grams brown sugar, firmly packed
2 tablespoons vegetable oil
2 eggs
120 ml. pumpkin (canned)
4 tablespoons raisins or dried currants, finely chopped

In a small bowl combine flour, baking powder and pumpkin pie spice; set aside. In a medium mixing bowl combine brown sugar and oil, and beat till well combined. Beat in eggs. Add pumpkin and mix well. Add flour mixture. Beat just until combined. Stir in raisins. Pour pumpkin mixture into 2 well-

RHUBARB MOUSSE

450 grams rhubarb; cut into 2-inch pieces
150 grams sugar
125 ml water
2 tablespoons butter
½ teaspoon vanilla essence
500 ml. double cream, whipped

Place the rhubarb in the slow cooker along with the sugar and water. Cover and cook on low setting for 6 to 8 hours. Remove the cover, turn off the heat, and stir in the butter and the vanilla. Drain away most of the juice. Fold the strained rhubarb into the unsweetened double cream, whipped. Turn into a serving bowl, cover, and chill for a few minutes in the freezer before serving.

RHUBARB BAKE

1.2 kg. fresh rhubarb
170 grams sugar
1 cinnamon stick
2 whole cloves
1 teaspoon grated lemon peel
60 grams flour or margarine
30 grams flour
90 grams sugar

Cut rhubarb into small pieces. Combine rhubarb with 135 grams sugar, cinnamon, cloves and lemon peel in slow cooker. Cover and cook on low setting for 3 to 4 hours. Remove whole spices. Spoon rhubarb into baking dish. Combine remaining ingredients and sprinkle over rhubarb. Bake in the oven at 400°F for 20 to 25 minutes. Serves 4 to 6.

RHUBARB CROCKPOT BETTY

2 kg. peeled rhubarb
220 grams sugar
3 tablespoons quick-cooking tapioca
1 tablespoon grated orange peel
¼ teaspoon salt
1 teaspoon vanilla
85 ml. melted butter
240 grams soft bread crumbs
optional: whipped cream, plain yogurt or vanilla ice cream

Put rhubarb, sugar, tapioca, peels and salt into slow cooker. Mix well. Combine vanilla and butter. Add crumbs and mix well. Distribute evenly over top of rhubarb. Cover and cook on high setting for about 2 hours. Serve warm with any of the optional ingredients.

RICE PUDDING

500 grams cooked rice
375 ml. scalded milk
160 grams white or brown sugar
3 eggs, beaten
1 teaspoon salt
2 tablespoon. vanilla
1 teaspoon cinnamon
1 teaspoon nutmeg
115 grams raisins
3 tablespoon. soft butter

Combine all ingredients. Pour into lightly greased crockpot. Cook on high setting for 1 to 2 hours. Stir during first 30 minutes. Recipe can be doubled.

RICH BROWNIES IN A NUT CRUST

60 grams butter or margarine, melted
150 grams chopped nuts
1 family-size packet brownie mix (about 650 grams)

Pour melted butter into 2-pound coffee can; swirl to butter sides. Sprinkle with half the nuts. Mix brownies according to the packet directions. Pour half the batter into coffee can, covering nuts evenly. Add remaining half of nuts, then batter. Place can in crockpot. Cover top of can with 8 paper towels. Cover and cook on high setting for 3 hours. Do not check or remove cover until last hour. Remove can and discard paper towels. Allow to stand for 5 minutes. Unmould and serve warm. Makes 24 brownies

RUM-BUTTERSCOTCH BANANAS

125 ml. unsalted butter
100 grams firmly packed light brown sugar
65 ml. dark rum
2 large firm ripe bananas
    vanilla ice cream

Add the first 3 ingredients to a slow cooker; stir to combine. Cover and cook on low setting for 1 to 1½ hours. Stir with a whisk until smooth. Just before serving, peel the bananas; cut in half lengthwise, and cut each piece in half crosswise to make 4 pieces per banana. Add to the hot sauce. Cover and continue to cook on low setting until heated through and coated with the sauce (15-20 minutes). Serve immediately over scoops of vanilla ice cream. Serves 4.

SPICED APPLES IN WINE

6 tart cooking apples
1 cup red wine or cranberry juice
½ cup granulated sugar
¼ teaspoon ground nutmeg
½ teaspoon ground cinnamon
1/8 teaspoon black pepper (optional)
2 slices fresh lemon

Core, peel, and quarter apples. Combine wine, sugar in crockpot, stir well. Add apple quarters. Stir well to coat apples with wine mixture. Add nutmeg, cinnamon, pepper and lemon slices. Cover and cook on high setting for 2 to 3 hours. Transfer apples and liquid to a refrigerator container and chill well. Serve in sorbet glasses. Serves 8.

RICE PUDDING WITH FRUIT

1.9 litres milk (or substitute with evaporated milk for a very rich flavour)
225 grams uncooked rice
200 grams sugar
3 tablespoons cold margarine
¼ teaspoon salt, optional
1 teaspoon vanilla essence
75 grams dried apricots or peaches, minced
¼ teaspoon ground cinnamon

The cooking time will vary greatly, anywhere from 1½ to 3½ hours. The longer it cooks, the thicker it will be. It is important to have the dried apricots minced. Put all ingredients into the slow cooker, and stir to blend well. Cover and cook on high setting for 1½ hours. Stir once after about an hour. Or, cook on high setting for the first 30 minutes, then turn to low setting and cook as long as desired. Check after the first 2 hours of low cooking and stir. If the rice is not absorbing the milk quickly enough, turn the slow cooker up to high again. Keep cover on at all times. Slow Cooker temperatures vary widely among different brands. Only with experimentation can tell you the correct amount of time for cooking in your slow cooker. Rarely will a slow cooker recipe fail, though, as the long, slow cooking process does not require precise timing. Serves 8.

RICOTTA AMARETTO CHEESECAKE

Crust:
120 grams vanilla wafer crumbs (about
21 to 23 cookies)
1 tablespoon sugar
1/8 teaspoon almond essence
3 tablespoons butter

Filling:
425 grams light ricotta cheese
225 grams cream cheese
170 grams sugar
3 large eggs plus 1 egg yolk
60 ml. Amaretto liqueur
2 tablespoons all-purpose flour
1/4 teaspoon almond essence
1/2 teaspoon vanilla essence

Combine crust ingredients well; pat into a 7-inch cake tin. Beat sugar into the cheeses; add eggs; beat for 2 to 3 minutes on medium speed of an electric hand-held mixer. Add remaining filling ingredients and beat about 2 minutes more. Pour into prepared crust. Place the cheesecake on a rack in the crockpot (or use a "ring" of aluminium foil to keep it off the bottom of the pot). Cover and cook on high setting for 2½ to 3 hours. After turning off the crockpot, allow it to stand in the covered pot for about 1 to 2 hours, until cool enough to handle. Cool thoroughly before removing pan sides. Chill before serving; store leftovers in the refrigerator.

SLOW-COOKER CANDY

907 grams white almond bark
115 grams bar German chocolate
340 grams chocolate chips
680 grams dry roasted peanuts

Put all ingredients in crockpot, and cook for one hour on high setting. Do not stir. Turn crockpot to low setting and stir every 15 minutes for 1 hour. Drop onto greaseproof paper and cool. Store in an air-tight container.

SWEET POTATO AND PINEAPPLE PUDDING

1.36 kg. sweet potatoes, peeled and grated
2 x 225 gram cans crushed pineapple in unsweetened juice (do not drain)
1 x 340 gram can evaporated milk
250 grams brown sugar, firmly packed
6 tablespoons margarine or butter, cut in cubes
3 eggs, slightly beaten
1 tablespoon ground cinnamon
½ teaspoon nutmeg

Lightly grease a large crockpot. In crockpot combine sweet potatoes, pineapple, evaporated milk, brown sugar, margarine, eggs, cinnamon, and nutmeg. Cover and cook on low setting for 7 to 8 hours or on high setting for 4 hours, stirring every 2 hours until the potatoes are tender. Serve hot or at room temperature.
NOTE: This dish may appear to be curdling, however it will come together toward the end of the cooking. Serves 10 to 12.

SPOON PEACHES

90 grams sugar
100 grams brown sugar
2 teaspoon margarine, melted
½ can evaporated milk
170 grams Bisquik
2 eggs
500 ml. peaches, mashed
2 teaspoon vanilla
¾ teaspoon cinnamon

Spray slow cooker with non-stick cooking spray. Combine sugars and Bisquik. Add eggs and vanilla. Add margarine and milk. Add peaches and cinnamon. Pour into slow cooker, and cook on low setting for 6 to 8 hours.

SPICED PEACHES IN BRANDY

3 large peaches, sliced
2 tablespoons brown sugar
1 cinnamon stick
1 pinch nutmeg
2 whole cloves
85 ml. brandy

Combine all ingredients and put into crockpot. Cook for 2 to 3 hours until peaches are tender. Remove cloves and cinnamon stick. Chill 1 hour before serving. Sauce will thicken. Serves 4.

STRAWBERRY PUDDING

1 can strawberry pie filling
1 packet strawberry cake mix
125 ml. melted butter or margarine
60 grams chopped black walnuts
Instant whip

Place pie filling in crockpot. Combine dry cake mix and butter thoroughly, using fingers if necessary. The mixture will be crumbly. Sprinkle over the filling. Sprinkle walnuts evenly over the top. Cover and cook on low setting for 2 to 3 hours. Serve in bowls topped with a dollop of instant whip. Serves 8.

SUGARED WALNUTS AND PECANS

450 grams pecans or walnut pieces
120 grams unsalted butter, melted
120 grams icing sugar
¼ teaspoon ground mixed spice
1/8 teaspoon ground cloves
1½ teaspoons ground cinnamon
¼ teaspoon ground ginger

Preheat slow cooker on high setting for 15 minutes. First, in preheated slow cooker stir the walnuts (or pecans) and butter until mixed well. Add the icing sugar, stirring to coat evenly. Cover and cook on high setting for 15 minutes. Reduce the heat to low setting and continued to cook, uncovered, stirring occasionally, until the nuts are coated with a crisp glaze (should be after about 2 hours.) Transfer the nuts to a bowl. In another small bowl, combine the spices and sift them over the nuts, stirring to coat evenly. Allow to cool before serving.

SUGARED PECANS

450 grams pecan halves
120 grams butter, melted
120 grams icing sugar
1 1/2 teaspoons ground cinnamon
1/4 teaspoon ground ginger
1/4 teaspoon ground mixed spice

Stir the pecans and butter in a large crockpot until combined. Add icing sugar, stirring to coat. Cover and cook on high setting for 15 minutes. Turn to low setting and cook uncovered for about 2 hours, or until the nuts are covered with a crisp glaze. Transfer to a bowl, combine spices and sift over nuts, tossing to distribute evenly. Cool before serving.

SWEET POTATOES WITH APPLES

5 medium sweet potatoes
3 Granny Smith apples, peeled, cored and cut in wedges
¼ teaspoon ground nutmeg
¼ teaspoon ground cinnamon
60 ml. maple flavoured syrup
2 tablespoons butter, melted
60 grams pecan pieces

Generously grease the bottom and sides of the slow cooker with butter or margarine. Peel sweet potatoes; cut into ½ inch slices. Place on bottom of slow cooker. Top with apple wedges; then nutmeg and cinnamon, maple syrup, and the melted butter. Cover and cook on low setting for about 4 hours or until potatoes are tender. Sprinkle with pecans in the last 30 minutes. Serves 4 to 6.

SWEET SWEET-POTATOES

900 grams sweet potatoes, peeled and grated
90 grams brown sugar, well-packed
60 grams flour
60 grams coconut, flaked
60 grams broken pecans, toasted
¼ teaspoon cinnamon
¼ teaspoon coconut essence
¼ teaspoon vanilla

Combine potatoes, sugar, butter, coconut, pecans and cinnamon in a slow cooker. Cover and cook on low setting for 6 to 8 hours or on high setting for 3 to 4 hours. Stir in coconut and vanilla essences

TRIPLE CHOCOLATE MESS

1 packet chocolate cake mix
500 ml. sour cream
1 packet instant chocolate pudding (any size)
450 grams chocolate chips
190 ml. oil
4 eggs
250 ml. water

Spray crockpot with non-stick spray. Mix all ingredients. Cook on low setting for 6 to 8 hours. Try not to lift the lid. Serve with ice cream.

ZUCCHINI BREAD

2 eggs
170 ml. vegetable oil
250 grams sugar
225 grams zucchini, peeled and grated
2 teaspoons vanilla
500 grams self-raising flour
1/4 teaspoon salt
1/2 teaspoon baking powder
1 teaspoon cinnamon
1/2 teaspoon nutmeg
250 ml. chopped nuts

Beat eggs until light and foamy with mixer. Add oil, sugar, grated zucchini and vanilla. Mix well. Stir dry ingredients with nuts. Add to zucchini mixture. Mix well. Pour into greased and floured 2 pound coffee can or 2 quart mould. Place in crockpot, and cover top with 8 paper towels. Cover and bake on high setting for 3 to 4 hours. Do not check or remove cover until last hour of baking. All to stand for 5 minutes before removing from mould.

Printed in Dunstable, United Kingdom

74891999R00083